GREAT WOMEN-SINGERS OF MY TIME

BY
HERMAN KLEIN

WITH A FOREWORD BY
ERNEST NEWMAN

WITH SIXTEEN PORTRAITS

NEW YORK

E. P. DUTTON & COMPANY

1931

TIETJENS AS LUCREZIA BORGIA

A

CONTENTS

v

A

A

LIST OF ILLUSTRATIONS

FOREWORD

MR KLEIN is of the opinion that on the whole the singers of to-day are not the equals of those of thirty to seventy years ago. It is easy to turn that off with a smile and a quotation of *laudator temporis acti;* but we would do well to reflect that Mr Klein has more right to his opinion than we have to the contrary one, for while he has heard all our crack singers, the majority of us have heard very few of his. It is not everyone's memory that can go back in music for something over sixty years; not everyone who can recall, for instance, having heard Tietjens in 1866. While Mr Klein has taken all music for his province—as befitted the one-time critic of the *Sunday Times*—he has always been particularly interested in singing; and I know of no other living writer who is so equipped to tell us of the vocal glories of the past and to compare them with those of to-day.

That the story is worth telling no one who has read the following pages can doubt. As Mr Klein says, it is a pity the gramophone was not invented a few generations earlier than it was. We might then have been able to hear the great singers of the past for ourselves, and to get some faint idea of what the Fidelio of Schroeder-Devrient was like, or Nilsson's Donna Elvira, or Tietjens' Donna Anna, or Materna's Brynhilde, or Ilma di Murska's Queen of Night, or

Malten's Kundry, or to know what Patti sounded like in her best days. It stands to reason that our fathers and grandfathers would not have raved as they did over these and other singers unless they were something quite out of the common; and to be out of the common, one suspects, meant more in the singing world of that time than it does in ours, for the standard was higher.

It was an age when singing, *qua* singing, counted for relatively more in opera than it does now, and that for two reasons. In the first place, the singing itself, we can hardly doubt, was technically better than ours; and in the second place, the singer himself counted for relatively more in the total effect, and the work for relatively less, than is the case now. In these days we may admire our singers, but we do not worship them; for a journalist even to speak of a soprano as a *diva* is to raise a smile. The reasons for this decline of the singer in the general estimation are manifold. This is an unromantic age, and singers are too plentiful, and for the most part too much on the one level, for us to feel much wonder at them. Other stars have latterly swum into the firmament of the populace—the film star, the tennis star, the aviation star and a score of others have pushed the *diva* off her historic throne. It might even be debated whether the passing of the singer as a romantic object is not due to the invention of the motor car. The romantic impulses of the crowd could find an outlet in the old days by unyoking the horses of the prima donna's carriage and drawing her in triumph to her hotel. The supersession of the horse by the dynamo has changed all that: we could not conceive the most excited of students taking the sparking-plug out of the diva's Rolls-Royce and dragging the car, with her in it, to the Ritz. Not until the horse comes back, perhaps, shall we find humanity again making an ass of itself over the prima donna.

There have been other reasons for the change of sentiment. The Press Agent and the gossipy journalist, without intending it, have made the singer a trifle ridiculous; the plain man finds it hard to take people seriously about whom so much vulgar nonsense is talked. Not that the old-time singers and actors were, as a class, of the shrinking violet kind. They were as vain as most musicians are to-day, and we may be sure they welcomed everything that ministered to their vanity. But apparently in those days there were limits. With the present-day type of singer and actor before us in all his absurdity, it is hard to believe that there was ever a time when the fauna had still so much natural decency and dignity left as to shrink from publicity of the vulgarer kind. Yet so it was, seemingly, with the great operatic artists of the mid-nineteenth century. It is refreshing to read, in Mr Klein's pages, that Jenny Lind, when she got to America and realized by what methods Barnum meant to exploit her, was so annoyed that she wanted to cancel her contract with him; and it is at once sad and, in a way, refreshing, to read that her disgust with the new methods of publicity was so profound as to accelerate her retirement into private life. The modern prima donna, for commercial reasons, has come down into the crowd; and too close contact with the crowd has meant the loss of a good deal of the crowd's respect for her.

Mr Klein hints at yet another reason for the relative

decline of the singer in public esteem. The work and the composer have come to mean more to the audience than he does, no matter how great he may be. This change must be put down mostly to Wagner's account; Mr Klein, indeed, fixes upon the year 1882 as a sort of dividing line. When the critics were face to face only with a "Lucia di Lammermoor", a "Robert the Devil", or a "Norma", it was natural that they should devote their notices mainly to the art of the great singers who appeared in them. But after a little acquaintance with works like "Tristan" and the "Ring" and the "Meistersinger", the critics discovered that even the greatest of singers mattered much less than the work itself. The centre of critical and of public interest gradually shifted, with the result that to-day the operatic singer is judged less for what he is in himself than for what he contributes, or fails to contribute, to the realization of the dramatic purpose of the composer. We prefer a good singer to a bad one, of course; but we insist on even the best singing being placed at the service of the composer rather than put forward as a rival to him or a substitute for him.

Yet it would be a mistake to think, as most of us have been inclined to do at one time or another, that the great singers of the past were merely superb vocal instruments, bent solely on individual display, without any regard for, or any sense of the dramatic meaning of, the work as a whole. We must not be misled by some of the more palpable absurdities of the period and of the genre; we must learn to see these things in historical perspective. We may smile at the stories of Patti refusing to attend rehearsals, and of her even sending her agent Strakosch to represent her at some of these. But there were operas of the older school to which no great harm could be done, even from the purely dramatic point of view, by an attitude of this kind; while there is abundant evidence that for the most part the great singers took a really serious dramatic idea with all possible seriousness. It is always a fair assumption that our fathers were no bigger fools than we are; and it is hardly likely that intelligent listeners would have gone into the ecstasies they did over the Fidelio of this singer, the Valentine of that, the Alice of a third, or the Selika of a fourth, unless the players of these rôles had been intelligent actors as well as fine singers. On points like this we may accept the verdict of Mr Klein, who has had unequalled opportunities for comparing the operatic singers of that day with those of the present; and when he tells us, for instance, that the Fidelio of Tietjens "more than matched the Fidelios of Ternina, Hastreiter, and Lilli Lehmann at their best", we may reasonably believe that while the general standard of operatic acting may have risen since the 1860's—thanks to the reforms of Wagner and the new dramatic consciousness with which he endowed not only the actors but the public—the great singers of that day were in many cases the equals of our own as actors as well as their superiors as singers. It may even be that Wagner and his successors have made things too easy for the artists; the proposition might be sustained that to a large extent the work of the Brynhilde or the Isolde or the Aida of the evening has been already done for her by the composer—especially in the orchestra—while the Norma or the Selika or the Alice of the old days had to rely infinitely more on herself.

There can be little doubt, I think, that the singers who brought the world to their feet in such rôles as these would have done even better in the great modern parts. It will not escape the attentive reader of Mr Klein's pages that more than one of his subjects actually achieved triumphantly the transition from the older musical and dramatic art to the new. We seem to be in another operatic world than ours when we read how Tietjens, in Dublin, sang " The Last Rose of Summer ", to the accompaniment of a piano that had been dragged on to the stage, as an encore to the big aria in " Oberon "—" Ocean, thou mighty monster ". Yet this same Tietjens lived to be a remarkable Ortrud; and many another great Wagner singer of the 1880's and 1890's had graduated in the school of the older Italian opera. It cannot, then, have been so bad a school of acting as we are sometimes apt to believe.

Mr Klein has done us a great service in setting down his reminiscences of the singers of the past. It is not merely that the story is an interesting one in itself; the reminiscences are valuable for the light they throw on another musical civilization than our own, and one that we are too accustomed to look down upon. It will do us a lot of good to realize that, operatically speaking, we of the present day are not the lords of creation we imagine ourselves to be, and that, all in all, our fathers lost little by not having postponed their birth half-a-century or so. If we of to-day have gained something on the swings, we have certainly lost something on the roundabouts. On what stage in the world to-day could we hope to hear such a cast in " Don Giovanni " as the London one of 1869, with Tietjens as Donna Anna, Nilsson as Donna

Elvira, Faure as Don Giovanni, Mario as Don Ottavio, and Patti as Zerlina? It only needed Eclipse as the horse in the cemetery scene to complete an ideal cast!

ERNEST NEWMAN.

GREAT WOMEN-SINGERS OF MY TIME

CHAPTER I

THE VICTORIAN PRIMA DONNA

THIS book deals with the lives and careers of the great women-singers whom I have heard. It was my good fortune not only to hear but to know personally most of these celebrities of the Victorian era when they were in their prime. I shall now endeavour to describe them and their voices and give a critic's impression of the qualities that made them remarkable.

It was, in a sense, my duty to undertake this task. As one grows older—and I am now the doyen of English musical critics—one's youthful recollections of voices and personalities are apt to fade. They ought, therefore, to be recorded before they become blurred and hazy. During a lifetime spent in listening to singers—good, bad, and indifferent—I have heard an illustrious few of whom it may be said, without fear of contradiction, that " we shall ne'er look upon their like again ".

To the present generation they can be little more than names. Electrical recording was invented too late for the gramophone to preserve accurately the sound of their voices, their idiosyncrasies of style, or their amazing technique. The earlier records were not really worthy of the two or three celebrities who made them. The printed page is, I fear, a poor substitute for the real thing, since language is at any time inadequate to express the wonder of a beautiful voice and glorious singing.

It was the custom for the older musical writers from whom I learned my craft to expatiate lengthily upon the methods, the " airs and graces ", the tonal qualities and executive triumphs of the operatic favourites of the moment. *Autres temps, autres mœurs.* The music critic of to-day refuses, and with good reason, to wax eloquent over the heroines of old-fashioned Italian opera. He feels that his readers are more interested in Brünnhildes and Isoldes than in Rosinas and Lucias. Quite right, too; yet I often think that, at a time when the art of singing has palpably declined, it might be beneficial to discuss it more patiently. For, to be reliably informed about the achievements of genius, to learn the truth concerning the phenomenal gifts of accomplished singers of a notable epoch, whatever their particular branch, is to obtain access to a fount that may yield inspiration or even lead to a sharpening of ideals for all who are interested or working in this great art.

Prior to the eighties, if one knew where to look, there were plenty of biographies to be found of celebrated *prime donne* who flourished during the early Victorian era. You could feast upon the chronicles of Lord Mount Edgcumbe, the wealthy amateur; of Henry Chorley, the astute, well-informed critic; of Dr John Cox, the amiable *dilettante;* of Benjamin Lumley, the dignified impresario of Her Majesty's

Theatre. You could have read volumes of gossip concerning the intrigues, the struggles, the mistakes, and withal the triumphs and disappointments of famous women like Catalani, Mara, Pasta, Malibran, Sontag, Giulia Grisi, Persiani, and Jenny Lind. But these last were stories connected with operatic events that happened best part of a century ago.

The cycle I am dealing with marked the close of the Golden Age of the lyric art. I watched its slow *Dämmerung* and observed with sorrow the final procession of the goddesses into Valhalla. To be exact, of course, there was only one *diva* at the finish, just as there was only one Fricka. The title was created in the thirties for Giulia Grisi, and descended from her to Adelina Patti, whose coming (in 1861) had synchronized with the elder singer's farewell. Even during the hectic years of the " Jenny Lind fever " it was Grisi alone who was spoken of as the " *diva* ". Patti bore the title until the day of her death, half a century later, though the *hoi polloi* preferred to call her the " Queen of Song ".

Such distinctions have less value in these less hero-worshipping days. As a matter of fact, I recall them only because they are redolent of the period that invented them. But there were others—great singers also—who were content to do without a handle to their honoured names ; and, inasmuch as it was not the fashion then for retired *prime donne* to write their reminiscences (or get someone to do it for them), one may seek in vain for their biographies beyond the crowded pages of *Grove* or some other musical dictionary. As it is, I have been unable to find room for all, or nearly all, of those who were entitled alike by talent and reputation to be called " goddesses " and to sit upon the steps of the Olympian throne (if there be such a thing in Valhalla).

Yet, if they are perforce omitted from these pages, I have not forgotten such splendid French singers of 1870–1900 as Miolan Carvalho, Marie Marimon, Galli-Marié, Marie Rôze, Gabrielle Krauss, Cécile Simonnet, Rose Caron, Hélène Richard, Lucienne Bréval, Marie Delna, Marie Deschamps-Jéhin, Meyriane Héglon, Marie Ugalde,—nearly all of whom sang in opera in London; nor our English Lemmens-Sherrington, and Marie Brema, both as admirable in opera as they were in oratorio; nor the brilliant American and Scandinavian " stars ", Minnie Hauk, Sigrid Arnoldson, Emma Nevada, Aino Ackté, Zélie de Lussan, Marie Vanzandt, Ella Russell, Emma Eames, Alwina Valleria, Maria Durand, Suzanne Adams, Louise Homer; nor such ornaments of the Italian stage as Etelka Gerster, Bianca Bianchi, D'Angeri, Sessi, Sinico, Zaré Thalberg, Anna de Belocca, and Caroline Salla.

All of these I heard; and the majority were remarkable enough to have deserved something beyond mere mention. But I am reserving what space there is left for the great Wagnerian singers who visited London from time to time, during the years that elapsed between the beginning of the Bayreuth movement and the close of the century. For they likewise are in danger of being forgotten.

It is not among the objects of this book merely to praise the past or draw comparisons disparaging to the present. If we have gone back in some respects, we have gone forward in others. What has been loss for opera and oratorio has been gain for orchestral and chamber music, and perhaps for the art of Lieder-singing. Let the balance stand level at that. *Plus ça change, plus c'est la même chose.* In art there must be development or there will be no progress. The fundamental principles remain unaltered and unalterable. Actually, the only novel growth in the psychology of to-day's prominent singers centres in the business of self-advertisement.

You may ask, "Did all these wonderful women whom we are going to read about do without a press-agent?" Yes; for the simple reason that when they flourished the individual in question had not been invented. What advertising there was to be done had to be left entirely to the impresario. There was no *tertium quid* in those days!

I do not say that the average *prima donna assoluta* was disinclined to improve the occasion when a bit of gossip came along or a *suggestio falsi* on the part of a rival had to be contradicted. It is also practically certain that her weakness for conversation with distinguished journalists acted as a stimulus to the popular growth of the "interview". Still, I repeat, and to her credit be it said, she did not as a rule trouble the world by publishing her reminiscences.

The whole system of operatic and theatrical self-advertisement was inspired by the example of the American showman, Barnum. Until Jenny Lind went to the United States under the *aegis* of that shrewd manager the two types had never come into contact. A sensitive nature such as hers must have shrunk from the new experience. Her accompanist and friend, Sir Julius Benedict, once told me that her first impulse when she discovered the nature of Barnum's policy, was to break her contract and take the first steamer back to Europe. But wiser thoughts prevailed. She had to content herself with imploring Barnum to use no superlative descriptions of her in the bills and to keep her out of sight as much as possible. He agreed, of course, but did not keep his word. Jenny Lind never recovered from her horror of this exploitation of the woman as well as the artist, and its effect was to intensify the dislike of public life which eventuated in her premature retirement.

The idolized cantatrice of the twentieth century is not worried by this excessive aversion from the consequences of calculated publicity. She no longer indulges in an " annual benefit ", with bouquets hurled upon the stage from all parts of the house; she accepts instead, with graceful *élan*, an endless array of colossal floral devices as they are handed up to the platform of the Albert Hall. No longer, either, may she feel the pride and excitement of having her carriage dragged by a crowd of noisy students, after the performance, from the stage-door to her hotel amid a torchlight procession,—the whole demonstration carefully organized by her impresario. But she can always pose as the *grande dame* at Society functions, mayoral banquets, charity entertainments, and so forth; beating even the actresses at the game of getting her name and pictures into the papers. " And so she plays her part."

The prima donna as a type still exists; and always will exist, of course, so long as opera, her natural element, continues to provide her with a *raison d'être*. But the personality of her proud Victorian prototype seems to have vanished, along with her other incomparable gifts. Nevertheless, these pages are not supposed to portray a race of superior beings. No; they deal simply with a group of supreme artists, some of whom were very marvellous singers. And that, I hope, will suffice.

CHAPTER II

THERESA TIETJENS

TRUE SUCCESSOR TO JENNY LIND

I

IF Jenny Lind had a veritable successor it was assuredly that great dramatic soprano, Theresa Tietjens. If the fact be not commonly recognized, it is because Jenny Lind, who was the older artist, outlived Tietjens by ten years, having—although she continued for a long while to adorn the concert platform—retired from the operatic stage so far back as May, 1849, *i.e.*, nine years before Tietjens made her first appearance in this country. Time was to prove, however, that the newcomer united in herself the whole of the rare qualities—the genius for oratorio as well as opera, together with the personal attributes that command the affection and esteem of a nation—which could justify the claim that she was the true successor of Jenny Lind. I will venture to add that both as an artist and a woman she was her equal.

I heard Jenny Lind once, when a boy of seven, at a concert given at St. Andrew's Hall, Norwich (my birthplace); but I cannot now recollect what her voice was like—only that it sounded very beautiful and marvellously pure. Three years later, in the same hall, I heard Tietjens for the first time at a rehearsal of the

Messiah for the Norwich Festival,[1] and I still recall her singing of " Rejoice greatly " as though it had been yesterday. How could one ever forget those liquid, coruscating runs or such splendidly vigorous declamation! Surely, if Jenny Lind's was the ideal " I know that my Redeemer liveth ", here was the ideal " Rejoice greatly "; and, indeed, such was the opinion of many who were able to compare the two.

My own boyish impression was that the tall, stately woman who was wearing at rehearsal a plain walking costume with the ample skirts of the mid-sixties, must have been an absolutely heaven-born oratorio singer. Then in London, after 1869, I heard Tietjens more than once at Exeter Hall in the *Messiah* and *Elijah* (superb in " Hear ye, Israel ") and also at the Handel Festival of 1874 in, among other things, the air from *Susannah*, " If guiltless blood be your intent ". From first to last there was always in these efforts the same unfailing dignity and nobility of style, the same vocal grandeur, the same purity and breadth of phrasing and clarity of diction. Everything, in fact, that could lend an added beauty and significance to the music of these immortal masterpieces.

2

Theresa Tietjens was born of Hungarian parents at Hamburg, on July 17, 1831; and in that city she made her first appearance at the age of 18, at the St. Pauli Theatre, as Irma in Auber's pretty opera *Le Maçon*. Her remarkable promise secured for her a prompt engagement at Altona (a suburb of Hamburg), where

---

[1] This was in 1866, as stated in my *Thirty Years of Musical Life in London*, not in 1863, as I inadvertently wrote in *Musicians and Mummers*.

she made her real stage début at the State Opera House in October, 1849, as Lucrezia Borgia.[1] The fame of the new soprano spread quickly through Germany, and offers reached her from many places.

After gaining experience at Frankfort and other towns, she proceeded in 1856 to the Hofoper at Vienna, where she was hailed as the successor of the celebrated Henriette Sontag. Two years later she was engaged for London by Benjamin Lumley, the director of Her Majesty's Theatre, who had journeyed to Vienna expressly to hear her. He relates in his *Reminiscences of the Opera* how anxious he was to secure her, after a fruitless endeavour to do so in the previous season, and adds : " I heard Mademoiselle Tietjens sing once more, with newly-added advantages, and was delighted ".[2]

Her début at Her Majesty's on April 13, 1858, appears to have been a very exciting affair. Incidentally it rescued Mr Lumley for a time from financial disaster. Let us hear then, what he says about this, the opening night of the season, when Queen Victoria and Prince Albert were in the Royal box and the house was packed with a brilliant audience :

" The production of the *Huguenots* (for the first time at this house) with the new and much-anticipated prima donna

---

[1] This rôle she practically made her own, and she appeared in it at Her Majesty's Theatre on the last night she ever sang.

[2] It should be noted that Lumley in his book retains the original and correct spelling of the name, Tietjens. In this country all through her career it was spelt " Titiens ", but, according to a footnote in Dr John Cox's *Musical Recollections*, " it was changed by Mr Lumley to assimilate it with that of the famous painter, Titian ". That may well have been the case, for most English people used to pronounce it so.

c

and the successful tenor of the previous year, Giuglini, was an event upon which the whole reputation of the theatre for the ensuing season, and the consequent fortunes of the establishment, might possibly depend. . . . To none were fame and fortune more at stake than to Mademoiselle Tietjens. As her powerful voice rang through the theatre and excited the plaudits of all present, so the latent fire of Giuglini[1] became kindled in its turn. . . . Both he and Tietjens were very nervous ; nevertheless the opera went off well, and the success of Tietjens and Giuglini was complete. I attended the Queen on her leaving her box, and she said to me, ' It was beautiful '. After the many absurd reports and the manner in which the Queen's name had been used, the visit was of great importance.

" The reception of Mademoiselle Tietjens was enthusiastic. Her splendid voice, her broad and impassioned style of acting, and her fine dramatic declamation all delighted her audience. The opera of the *Huguenots* maintained its position and its powers of attraction for many nights on the stage of Her Majesty's Theatre ; and with it was maintained also the fame of the striking prima donna who now first began to assert that supremacy which during many following years she continued to enjoy ".

3

Seventeen years later, at the outset of my journalistic career, I heard Tietjens for the first time at Drury Lane (the old Her Majesty's had been burned down

---

[1] It had been predicted that Giuglini's Raoul would be a failure ; that his lovely voice would not carry him through the opera, and that he would never be able to act the part. Lumley declares that he made a success in it, but elsewhere we read that the music of Raoul " lay ill for his voice and his action was unsuited " to the character. The latter verdict was the true one.

and the new one was not yet opened) in her unforgettable impersonation of Valentine. For me it was
an important event in more than one sense. The
great artist had herself sent me the ticket for the performance, as an acknowledgment of my " editorial "
courtesy in publishing her portrait in the *Operatic and
Dramatic Album*. I had already heard her as Norma,
Semiramide, Donna Anna, Pamina, and Leonora;
also, in 1872, at Drury Lane on the night of Campanini's début, as Lucrezia Borgia. And I always
thought her Norma the greatest embodiment of them
all.

But this performance of *Les Huguenots* was in 1875,
and Tietjens, then a woman of 44, had grown exceedingly stout. The disadvantage was partly compensated
for by her unusual height, by the remarkable dignity
of her carriage, and by her noble gestures. She was
not beautiful; yet one forgot the contour of the
features in the study of their mobile expression, the
glance of her intelligent eyes, the world of tenderness
in the loving smile that greeted a Gennaro, an Arsace,
or a Florestano. Above all, I sat entranced by the
rich, luscious tones that poured forth effortlessly in
the *grands duos* with Marcel and Raoul. One felt the
tragic intensity of situations that were undeniably
dramatic and of music no less charged with emotional
fervour.

For even then, despite some physical weakness,
Tietjens was still vocally in her prime. Her tones had
not lost any of their mellowness and power, nor the
strong, clear ring that distinguished every note of her
scale up to the high C—that amazing high C which
in the first finale, as Arditi has said in his *Reminiscences*
—on the night of her début " soared brilliantly above

the other voices and orchestra ". It did so again when I heard her, and brought forth a similar " roar and thunder of applause ".[1]

The slight physical unsuitableness just referred to did not prevent Tietjens from succeeding in several characters through sheer force of musical temperament, dramatic genius and magnificent singing. In the forefront of these I place her Fidelio. Its equal was said not to have been heard since the historic performance of Schröder-Devrient, whereof one can only speak on hearsay. My own estimate of Tietjens' is that it more than matched the Fidelios of Ternina, Hastreiter and Lilli Lehmann at their best. She had not the virginal charm for Agathe (*Der Freischütz*) nor the youthful grace for Martha ; and somehow, even Fidès (*Le Prophète*) did not display her finest qualities. But Mozart brought these out surely enough ; for her Donna Anna, her Countess, and her Pamina were in every respect magnificent. The first-named, like her

---

[1] William Kuhe has confessed that he might have devoted half a volume of his *Musical Recollections* to the memory of Tietjens, " one of the greatest artists and noblest women who ever trod the stage . . . not only because I consider her one of the truest artists of the century, but because she was one of the finest characters I have been privileged to know ". And after his meed of all-round praise, he frankly observes : " In the course of her long career there was, I think, only one among the parts she essayed for which she could be pronounced unfitted. This was the part of Marguerite in *Faust*, which she was the first to play on the (London) production of the work in 1863, when it was quite impossible to reconcile her tall and massive figure with the girlishness of an ideal Gretchen ". Tietjens, however, was far too sensible to cling to a part so obviously unsuited to her. She relinquished the new rôle to Christine Nilsson from the moment when that ideal Marguerite demonstrated her peculiar fitness for it.

Norma, was at moments terrible and overpowering in its outbursts of passionate rage.

If I never saw her in either of her great classical rôles, Medea or Iphigenia (*Tauride*), I had at least the good fortune to witness, at Drury Lane in 1875, one *tour de force* of her later days that stood out conspicuously. This was her superb Ortrud in Mapleson's Italian performance of *Lohengrin*, which had quickly followed upon Gye's first production at Covent Garden in May of the same year (*see* p. 107). Costa conducted; and the cast included Nilsson as Elsa and Galassi as Telramund, with Italo Campanini as Lohengrin.[1] The opera was utterly strange to most of the audience, and their amazement may be imagined when they saw their beloved "Teresa" (her public simply adored her) sitting or standing through the whole of the first act, without uttering a sound except to join in the prayer and finale. But though the music lay low for her voice, she quickly made up for her silence when the second act came. Her scolding of Telramund would have made Fricka's lecture to Wotan sound like gentle chiding; while, in her duet with a most bewitching Elsa, her *cantilena* vied with Nilsson's in lending to the "new music" an indescribably subtle fascination.

4

Her extraordinary versatility seems never to have astonished her public. "Tietjens", they were wont

---

[1] Mapleson, in his *Memoirs*, expresses his managerial gratitude by mentioning that "Mdlle Titiens very kindly undertook the rôle of 'Ortruda' and really excelled herself". I would add that her silence in the first act was not less eloquent than her declamation.

to say, "can sing anything, and no matter what it is that she does, she is equally great in all". One of her critics[1] remarked, "In oratorio Mdlle Titiens sang as finely as in opera; and she had not been many months in England when engagements were offered to her at our great provincial festivals".[2]

Certain fastidious critics of the sixties used to point out in Tietjens singularities of style that were, in their opinion, due to her German training. One in particular was specified as being distinctly un-Italian, namely, the curious jump or leap (not a "scoop") over an upward interval from the medium into the head register, making it sound something like an *acciaccatura*. I never heard any other singer do exactly the same thing in the same way; but even supposing it to have been a German trait, it was not in the least

---

[1] Mr Sutherland Edwards in his book, *The Prima Donna*.

[2] An interesting analysis of this phase of her art, from the pen of Mrs Julian Marshall, appeared in the second edition of *Grove's Dictionary*, but was omitted from the third. It is well worth quoting here:

"... She applied herself assiduously to the study of oratorio for which her services were in perpetual request. Perhaps the hardest worked singer who ever appeared, she was also the most faithful and conscientious of artists, never disappointing her public, who knew that her name on the bills was a guarantee against change of programme or apology for absence through indisposition. No doubt her splendid physique enabled her often to sing with impunity when others could not have done so, but her ceaseless efforts must have tended to break up her constitution at last. This great conscientiousness, as well as her genial, sympathetic nature, endeared her to the whole nation, and, though there never was a 'Tietjens fever', her popularity steadily increased and never waned. Her kindness and generosity to young and struggling artists and to her distressed countrymen knew no bounds, and became proverbial".

objectionable. It was always neatly executed, and clearly with intention. Only the purists drew attention either to this or any other ornament with which they were not familiar.[1]

She was invariably the bright particular star of Mapleson's provincial operatic tours, and it was during one of these—in 1874, whilst I was living in Liverpool—that I saw her in the round of her best characters already enumerated. I missed seeing her there in Weber's *Oberon*, but did so subsequently when the opera was revived in London. It was a delightful memory if only for her sublime rendering of " Ocean, thou mighty monster ! " By the way, a vivid story is related of the effect that her singing of this air had upon a Dublin crowd on the last night of the season in 1868 :

" The uproar lasted upwards of fifteen minutes before silence could be restored, when it was decided that ' The Last Rose of Summer ' should be given. But the orchestra had no music and the conductor would not venture a performance without it. Further delay and further uproar

[1] Dr John Cox (*Musical Recollections of the Last Half-Century*, Vol. II) was evidently one of the purists in question, albeit a whole-hearted admirer of Tietjens : " Here was indeed a genuine *artiste*, who, if she had only been taught after the Italian instead of the German method, would have been the greatest *prima donna* that had ever been heard—or heard of—since operatic music had sprung into existence. Even in the absence of that method she has held her ground as incomparable ; and at the present moment (1871), when her voice is approaching (*sic*) its decadence,—and no wonder, because of the wear and tear it has undergone, and the all but superhuman labours its possessor has undertaken and compassed, with an indomitable spirit and perseverance that nothing has ever daunted—there is not a single *artiste* that approaches her within the ' shadow of a shade ', or to take her place whenever she may retire ".

took place, until at length Signor Bettini, who had undertaken the rôle of Oberon, came from the wings, pulling on a cottage piano, whilst Titiens helped the conductor to get out of the orchestra in order to accompany her. As Bettini was turning the piano round, it fell right over, causing an immense cheer from the 'gods' when no less than five demons (who were to appear in the next scene of *Oberon*) rushed from the wings to raise it again on its legs (*sic*). No sooner had the singer finished the last verse than a roar of admiration was heard, so loud, so overpowering ", etc. . . .[1]

Then follows a description of how the Dublin students, after the opera was over, fixed ropes to her carriage and dragged it to the Shelbourne Hotel; how an enormous crowd gathered beneath her window and refused to disperse for over an hour (despite pouring rain and the fact that it was past midnight) until, at the request of the police she consented to come out on the balcony and sing " The Last Rose of Summer " over again—this time presumably without the hazardous support of the cottage piano with the groggy " legs ".

5

I should here mention that Mapleson was fond of dwelling on his bad luck in having allowed Adelina Patti to slip through his managerial fingers—" stolen from him by Frederic Gye " was his candid way of putting it. He might, with fairness, have expressed an equivalent measure of gratitude for the good fortune that had enabled him to secure the services of Theresa Tietjens for his brilliant London season at the Lyceum in June, 1861. He opened there with *Il Trovatore*, a

[1] *Mapleson Memoirs*, Vol. I.

wonderful " all star " cast, comprising Giuglini as
Manrico, Delle Sedie as the Conte di Luna, Gassier as
Ferrando, Alboni as Azucena, and Tietjens as Leonora.
The conductor was Arditi, who wrote, apropos of it,
" Titiens was at her very best; again triumphantly
proclaiming herself a brilliant Leonora, and doing
perfect justice to Verdi's music ". A few nights
afterwards the company won a race against Covent
Garden for the first production in England of Verdi's
new opera, *Un Ballo in Maschera*. With this the popular
soprano added Amalia to her répertoire, but not a
triumph to be compared with those she was then
achieving as Valentine, Norma, Lucrezia Borgia, and
Leonora.

Thenceforward for sixteen years—in other words,
to the end of her life—she faithfully and persistently
followed the varying fortunes of James Henry Mapleson. She appeared at Her Majesty's regularly every
season; also at Covent Garden during the wonderful
" Coalition " season of 1869.[1] It was not for lack of
trying that Mr Gye had failed long before then to
secure Tietjens for himself. But she had refused to be
tempted, and for that blessing her impresario was
apparently not ungrateful, seeing that in his earliest
prospectus at Her Majesty's (1862) he publicly acknowledged his debt to her in the following oddly-
chosen words :

" Of one [artist] a special word may not be out of place
since she may, without exaggeration, be said to constitute
the last link of that chain of glorious *prime donne* commencing

[1] That was when the two companies were combined at
Covent Garden under the dual control of Gye and Mapleson on
account of the opera house in the Haymarket having been
destroyed by fire.

with Catalani. It is seldom that Nature lavishes on one person all the gifts which are needed to form a great soprano: a voice whose register (*sic*) entitles it to claim this rank is of the rarest order. Melodious quality and power, which are not less essential than extended register, are equally scarce.[1] Musical knowledge, executive finish and perfect intonation (!) are indispensable, and to these the prima donna should add dramatic force and adaptability, together with a large amount of personal grace. Even these rare endowments will not suffice unless they are illumined by the fire of genius. By one only of living artists has this high ideal been reached—by Mdlle. Titiens ".

The above is worth quoting, despite its taint of managerial partiality, because it happened to be true. Sutherland Edwards, however, was obviously guilty of an exaggeration when he wrote in his book, *The Prima Donna*, " A certain number of characters may be said to die with Mdlle. Titiens ". Characters do not die (unless it be temporarily, on the stage). If the opera goes on living they must live too. Donna Anna, Fidelio and Norma are very much alive, and we have had in recent times some extremely fine interpreters of those parts. Whether they were so wholly satisfying as Tietjens is another question. In my opinion none of them has risen to the same extraordinary height of grandeur that she attained.

There was an impressive dignity that was not merely physical or due in any degree to technical accomplishment that seemed to lift Tietjens head and shoulders above her fellows. There was a beauty and distinction

[1] It is not difficult to perceive in this manifesto a sly and subtle shaft aimed indirectly at Patti, who had made her phenomenal début—not at Her Majesty's—in the previous year. A very long time was to elapse before Mapleson forgave her for eluding him.

of manner, linked with a purity of style, that peculiarly fitted her for opera of the pre-Romantic period and for the "classical" heroines of Mozart, Beethoven, Gluck, and Cherubini (*Medea*). The more distinguished her companions, the more brilliant her achievements appeared. Never shall I forget her amazing entry at the rise of the curtain in *Don Giovanni*. How grandly she "took the stage". How overpoweringly she turned upon her perfidious deceiver, both there and again in the ball-room scene. Then, finally, the nobility of her phrasing and exquisite tenderness of her inflections in "Non mi dir!" I never heard her in the historic cast of 1869, when she sang Donna Anna to the Don Giovanni of Faure, the Don Ottavio of Mario, the Donna Elvira of Christine Nilsson, and the Zerlina of Adelina Patti. But even in that celestial company she more than held her own.

6

Tietjens visited America for the first and only time late in 1876. Her health at that period was beginning to deteriorate, owing to the internal disorder which was ultimately to prove fatal. In the same year she sang at her last benefit concert at the Albert Hall, and among other things laid the first brick of Mapleson's projected National Opera House on the Embankment, where New Scotland Yard now stands.

After her return from the United States her physical condition improved for a few months, and she began her final season of 1877 at Her Majesty's, apparently in full possession of her powers. I heard her then in several operas, including Norma on the opening night, and also in *Lucrezia Borgia,* on what proved to be her last appearance upon the stage. This latter risk she undertook against the advice of her doctors, who desired to perform an operation at once ; but (it was on a Saturday night, the 19th May, 1877) she succeeded in persuading them to postpone their task until the following week.

The audience had little notion of the real state of affairs. Indeed, we should never have believed that a Lucrezia so glorious in every way was going through her part suffering pain at each step and every breath she took. Before the last act began someone told me that she had fainted twice during the evening. Then I watched more closely and could see that she was moving with difficulty. Moreover, her exclamation at the end when Lucrezia discovers that Gennaro is dead, had in it a ring that sounded like the cry of one in actual bodily pain. She sank to the stage more heavily than usual, and I was not surprised to learn that, after the curtain fell, she had remained where she had fallen insensible for twenty minutes. The public never saw or heard Tietjens again. After her fruitless operation she lingered on, suffering in patience, till the morning of October 3rd, when she passed peacefully away.

She was buried at the Kensal Green Cemetery, amid a display of mourning the like of which has never before or since paid tribute to a singer in this country. Fortunately I arrived early, or it would have been impossible to get near the little chapel where the simple service was held. The crowd was so vast that every avenue of approach was blocked. The small force of police on duty was quite unequal to the task of keeping such a throng in order. Nothing on a similar scale had been anticipated. There occurred tumultuous scenes of disorder so unprecedented that they gave rise to newspaper comment for days afterwards. Even whilst the coffin was being lowered into the grave the people rushed forward from every side, jumping recklessly over tombs and railings in the effort to obtain a last glimpse of the beloved remains. Fortunately no one was reported hurt.

7

Poor Tietjens ! A woman so modest would have preferred to go to her final resting-place amid a less unseemly demonstration, grateful though she might have been for the presence and the tears of thousands of the public that had requited her love with adoration. No wonder, then, that her death was accounted at the time a national loss ! The feeling of personal bereavement was widespread and profound in a degree that I have never known equalled, save in the case of some Royal or other great personage, political, naval or military.

Her career of less than twenty years in this country was a short one by comparison with those of some of her contemporaries. But, as Sutherland Edwards has truly said, " No one of the great *prime donne* became so thoroughly English as Mademoiselle Titiens at the time of her lamented death had become ".[1] To this result her character as a woman may be said to have contributed no less than her qualities as an artist. There was something very honest and genuine about her ; she created an atmosphere that was wholesome because it was utterly devoid of pretence or make-believe. She was singularly free from the foibles and caprices of her class.

[1] *The Prima Donna*, Vol. II, p. 55.

Her word could be relied upon because it was " as good as her bond ", and she never disappointed her public, even on account of illness, though it might have prolonged her life had she occasionally done so.

It was said that after her first season she never had a written contract with her manager (being in this respect as trustful as the de Reszkes were with Augustus Harris); and yet she was in most respects a thorough business woman. The famous conductor, Sir Michael Costa, who was the soul of punctuality, used to declare that Tietjens was the one prima donna upon whom he could always rely to be at rehearsal to the moment. She was likewise the only one to whose judgment he ever bowed. He knew what an excellent musician she was and had a sincere respect for her artistic opinions, to which she would give expression emphatically and without a moment's hesitation. In private life she was one of the kindest and most considerate of women. She had a charitable disposition, saved very little, and was invariably gracious to her fellow-artists.

CHAPTER III

ADELINA PATTI

" QUEEN OF SONG "

I

WHEN I first heard Patti at Covent Garden on the Whit-Monday of 1872, she had been married to the Marquis de Caux nearly four years. If not then referred to as the *diva*, it was quite customary for people to speak of her as the Marquise de Caux. Anyhow she was always addressed as " Marquise ", and as such she had become the most fêted and spoiled prima donna of her time. The high social position accorded her had not been without its effect upon her character ; but on the other hand it was never denied that she always retained her natural sweetness and amiability of manner. She was now, at the age of 29, at the very zenith of her powers, and this was her twelfth consecutive London season.

The opera was *Don Giovanni ;* and the cast was an extraordinary one, even for those days. In addition to Patti as Zerlina, it included the great French baritone Faure as the Don, Nicolini as Don Ottavio, the subsequently famous Marianne Brandt as Donna Elvira, Emmy Zimmerman as Donna Anna, and Ciampi as Leporello. But I had eyes and ears only for one entrancing singer, the captivating " little lady ", whom I now beheld for the first time. I was very young it is true, but I had already been to the opera often enough to be able to appreciate the musical qualities of such an exquisite Zerlina. Nor was it alone the indescribable beauty of her voice or the perfection of her Mozart singing that made her so alluring. Much might be attributable to the artless humour and vivacity of her acting. I could have testified there and then to the truth of Eduard Hanslick's opinion that she was " a born comédienne ".

Her full development as a serious actress did not, as a matter of fact, come until much later. Her precocious ability to play tragic parts like Valentine and Leonora when she was a mere girl had been due to her extraordinary powers of imitation. The impulse, the emotional energy did not come from within, but from her father. She would stand before him for hours watching his gestures and movements (he was rather a good actor) until she knew them as well as she knew her music, which, indeed, she learned in much the same way. In her case, however, imitation did not produce mechanical results alone. She absorbed exactly what she saw and heard, just as she had done when, as a child, she had been taken to see the operas that her parents sang. And what she " took in " she reproduced after her own fashion, stamped with an individuality and spontaneity peculiar to herself that grew and gathered force as the years went on.

When I next heard her, in 1875, as Gounod's Giulietta (the part she had created here in Italian to Mario's Roméo) the development had not gone far. If Mario had failed to inspire her, Nicolini could, apparently, do little more (although he was subsequently to become her husband in real life). The

PATTI AS AÏDA

manifest awakening was only perceptible at the Paris Opéra, thirteen years later, when she sang Juliette for the first time in French to the incomparable Roméo of Jean de Reszke.

In 1876 I was one of a serried crowd of enthusiasts who, after waiting for four hours on the gallery steps at Covent Garden, crushed in *en masse* (the *queue* being still unknown in London) to hear the first performance of *Aïda* in this country. Patti filled the title-rôle, Scalchi was the Amneris, Nicolini the Radamès, Cotogni the Amonasro, and Bagagiolo the Ramfis. It was a night of surprises in more senses than one. The novelty of the spectacle, the strange beauty of Verdi's unfamiliar harmonies, and the revelation of a new histrionic energy in Patti's picturesque assumption of the Ethiopian slave, were among the features that made us acclaim the occasion as a memorable one.

It is worth noting that *Aïda* was the only *new* opera that achieved enduring success at Covent Garden, out of the many that Patti sang in for the first time there. Apparently, no composer, however eminent, could contrive to write expressly for her a part in which she showed to genuine advantage. Always at her best in the older works of the Italian répertoire—in those of Mozart (though she never got beyond his *Don Giovanni*), Rossini, Bellini, Donizetti, and Verdi, in addition to some by Meyerbeer, Gounod, Auber, and Flotow—she herself was not the ablest judge of what would suit her. The greatest puzzle of all was her fixed belief that she could succeed as Carmen; and, oddly enough, the day before she made the attempt was the day on which I was first introduced to her.

D

2

It was in May, 1885. The Gyes were no longer in control at Covent Garden; the " Royal Italian Opera " was being directed by Col. Mapleson, now the diva's trusted impresario for America. She was staying together with Nicolini at the new Midland (St. Pancras) Hotel, in the Euston Road. I was taken there at her request by Louis Engel, the then-powerful musical critic of *The World*, who, by the way, used to play the harmonium *obbligato* for the Gounod " Ave Maria " at the Patti Concerts which periodically crammed the Royal Albert Hall.

She looked wonderfully youthful. Her smiling face, very little " made up ", and her *svelte* figure were those of a girl, although she had turned 42. (But neither then, nor at any time did it occur to me to reflect how old Patti might be. She always defied the years, and so long as I knew her the word " age " had no meaning for her.) She was in great spirits when she bade me welcome, for at that moment she was radiant with her new-found happiness—the first love romance she had ever known. Nicolini was there, of course, and he greeted me as an old friend, for we had met previously. He was, as always, extremely courteous and handsome.

" Are you coming to hear me in *Carmen?* " she asked, pointing to the yellow satin Spanish costume which was lying across the back of a chair. Naturally, I was; and just as naturally did she hope in her frank, jocular way, that I should " write a nice little article about her in the *Sunday Times* ", of which paper I had then been the critic for three or four years. Her low, resonant-speaking voice imparted a musical timbre to every syllable; and her English was without accent, despite an American idiom here and there. It seemed to me that, notwithstanding her eagerness to play Bizet's heroine, she was just a trifle anxious about her new part. If so, the sequel proved her to have been right. She was interested to learn that my grand old teacher, Manuel Garcia, had been seated beside me at the first London performance of *Carmen* at Her Majesty's Theatre seven years earlier. She had met him, I think, only once.

As she talked about Covent Garden and discussed its future prospects she grew more and more voluble, until at last Nicolini interfered with a warning that she was not to try her voice too much. At that I took my leave, telling her, as I did so, that she had made me the proudest young man in London.

But how, I was asking myself a couple of days later, could she ever have longed as she did to sing Carmen? What sort of appeal could the character drawn by Prosper Mérimée have offered to make it so irresistibly attractive to the naïve, candid disposition, the formal stage traditionalism, of Adelina Patti? Her acting, as I have already hinted, had improved considerably. Since her picturesque Aïda had revealed a capacity for simulating jealousy, some of her earlier impersonations had grown by inches; notably her Violetta, over which the greatest of "Dames aux Camélias", Sarah Bernhardt, had wept in Paris.

However, we had by then had other and more convincing Carmens of various types, from the wayward, capricious Minnie Hauk, the animalesque Pauline Lucca, and the burning Spanish Zélie de Lussan, down to the "lady-like" Carmencitas of Trebelli and Marie Roze. "Lady-like" was also the essential

adjective for Patti's Carmen. It was generally colourless and dull, including even her singing of the music,
which did not suit her. There was not a moment in
her whole performance that made my pulses beat
half so fast as her bewitching Zerlina had done
thirteen years before.

3

Adela Juana Maria Patti was born at Madrid on
February 10th, 1843. Her father, Salvatore Patti, was
a Sicilian and an operatic tenor. Her mother, *née*
Caterina Chiesa, whose first husband's name was
Barili, came of Roman and Venetian stock ; she was
an excellent dramatic soprano. This hard-working
woman on the eve of the date above-mentioned, sang
the part of Norma at the Royal Opera House, Madrid,
and had barely completed her stage task before another,
more real and even more serious, awaited her. There
was just time, however, for her to reach the Patti
lodgings before the latest addition to the family—
and by far the most important—came upon the scene.

Seven years afterwards that little girl was to sing
" by ear " Norma's great aria, " Casta diva ", at a
charity concert given in the city of New York (whither
the family had migrated), and instantaneously to earn
for herself a reputation as the most astounding vocal
prodigy that had ever appeared on the American
continent. · The tiny Adelina's precocious innate
talent, which forthwith became the means of rescuing
her people from poverty, had been as little suspected
by her parents as by her audience.

People listened in astonishment to her first childish
effort, made whilst standing upon a table on the platform of Tripler's Hall, New York, in the spring of

1850. Two men, however, took careful note of the event: one Max Maretzek, the organizer of the concert; the other, Maurice Strakosch, the husband of Amalia Patti, Adelina's eldest sister. As his father-in-law's partner, Strakosch was destined to unite in himself the functions of manager, factotum, coach, and impresario from that day forward until Adelina Patti married the Marquis de Caux on July 29th, 1868. Eighteen lucky years for Max!

But what a childhood for the girl! The whole family were singers or musicians of some sort. Amalia earned money as a vocalist; Carlotta, the second daughter, was a pianist at first and subsequently to become a famous concert soprano. The step-brother, Ettore Barili, was to be the little girl's first and practically (as she herself declared) her "only singing-teacher". It was true that she never needed instruction in the ordinary sense. Nature had not only given her a lovely voice, but taught her how to use it sanely, cleverly, even brilliantly, and with the utmost degree of effect.

Thanks to a miraculous ear, she could instantly repeat and remember whatever she heard; she could surmount without labour difficulties that took others hours and hours of study and hard striving. By the time Maurice Strakosch took her in hand at the age of seven, her mastery of vocal technique was well on the way to completion. Correct breathing, scales, shake, ornaments, *fiorituri* of every kind, all came naturally to her and required only the finishing touches. She just had to be shown the various *roulades* and cadenzas; to put them into her voice, as it were; then let them out again in a tone that resembled a nightingale's—pure, rich, luscious, warm, penetrating,

and of a haunting beauty. It grew with her from
childhood to womanhood, developing from year to
year with ever-increasing loveliness and power.

Whilst this was going on she was touring from city
to city, from State to State, from Canada in the North
to New Orleans in the South. Concerts she gave
everywhere with unvarying success ; sometimes alone,
but generally in conjunction with some well-known
instrumental artist—Gottschalk, the pianist, or Ole
Bull, the famous Norwegian violinist. She was
making money for the family, yet never spoilt by her
father or by Maurice Strakosch ; too used to applause
to be affected by it, she remained until she reached her
teens a veritable child. Her chief recreations were
dressing-up and play-acting ; but her principal, her
most enduring joy were her dolls ! Once at Cincinnati, she remained weeping in the artists' room and
refused to begin the concert till Strakosch brought
her a particular doll that he had promised her. There
was nothing for it but to go out and buy it. But the
moment it was hers she went on the platform happy,
and sang like a little angel.

For two years (from 1855 to 1857) she was not
allowed to do any work in public. Then, after one
more concert tour, Strakosch began the congenial
task of preparing her for the operatic stage.[1] Her
step-brother Barili, had prepared the way by teaching

---

[1] " Her voice was now settling down into a rich, lovely
soprano, clear and vibrant as a bell, especially in the head
register, which had a range extending easily to the F in *alt*.
The tone of the medium was not yet fully developed, but made
up in sweetness for what it lacked in power. The timbre and
character of the whole organ were singularly mature, distinctive
and individual ". (*The Reign of Patti*, p. 42.)

her the parts of Lucia, Amina, and Rosina; and she did further study on these and other rôles with Manzocchi, the conductor at the Academy of Music, New York, where she was to make her stage début.

4

That momentous event took place on November 24th, 1859, when Patti was in her seventeenth year. The opera was Donizetti's *Lucia di Lammermoor*, and she took the house by storm. Great things had been expected by her friends; "but great as their expectations were, they were far surpassed". The critics who only knew "Miss Patti" as a local singer of unusual promise, had the wit to recognize that there had arisen in their midst an opera singer of whose prodigious gifts New York was destined to be proud. During the prosperous season that followed she appeared in no fewer than fourteen operas, including *Lucia, Don Pasquale, L'Elisir d'Amore, Martha, Don Giovanni, Rigoletto, Ernani, Linda di Chamouni, La Traviata,* and *Il Trovatore.* Prodigious! Imagine Verdi's Violetta and Leonora sung by a girl of seventeen! Yet she was actually to add to these (at New Orleans) the two exacting Meyerbeer parts of Dinorah and Valentina (*Les Huguenots*); and she repeated them all, little and big, again and again, without evil consequences. Such things had never been accomplished in opera before.

Then, a year later, the tour over, came an event still more noteworthy, namely, the dazzling victory won over a critical phlegmatic London audience on the night of May 14th, 1861. The story of how this opportunity came about lies in a nutshell! Adelina

Patti, accompanied by Maurice Strakosch, had journeyed to England under engagement to Mr E. T. Smith through his agent, James Henry Mapleson, and was duly to have appeared at Her Majesty's Theatre. Her wily brother-in-law, however, discovering that financial difficulties had removed E. T. Smith from the operatic " cock-pit ", quickly transferred her services to Frederic Gye at Covent Garden ; and there, as Amina in *La Somnambula*, she made the most brilliantly successful début ever recorded in the history of the lyric stage.

A huge surprise was in store for everybody—including the impresario himself. An aristocratic assemblage enchanted by the strangely beautiful voice and exquisite singing of this youthful Amina, gradually abandoned their habitual reserve and gave her a welcome marked by unprecedented and unbounded enthusiasm. The radiant Adelina awoke next morning in her quiet hotel overlooking the Thames, to find herself famous.

We have in the circumstances of this extraordinary début—and the no less unparalleled eleven years' career as a prodigy which preceded it—the only explanation of Patti's instantaneous bound to the top of the tree. The phenomenal supremacy which she assumed in a night she held, however, against all comers down to her ultimate farewell ; and that is the great fact which differentiates Patti from the other great women-singers of the nineteenth century.

5

During her first year in England this tireless girl of 18—singing at Covent Garden under contract for an average fee or *cachet* of £32 10s. a performance, but elsewhere at a higher figure—was allowed only a brief summer holiday. She sang in London 25 times in 6 operas in 11 weeks, the operas being *La Somnambula, Lucia, La Traviata, Don Giovanni, Martha*, and *Il Barbiere di Siviglia*. The merry, raven-haired maiden, with her bright eyes and winning smile, also appeared in June amid the solemnities of a State Concert at Buckingham Palace, side by side with "Titiens", Giuglini, Gardoni, and Santley; taking part among other things, in a selection from Mendelssohn's *St. Paul*. She was next engaged that summer at a fee of 500 guineas for three concerts at the Birmingham Festival, under Costa.[1] She also sang for William Kuhe at one of his Brighton Concerts; she appeared in opera at Dublin and elsewhere in the provinces; and she began at Berlin in November the long series of "peregrinations in Europe" as Maurice Strakosch termed them, which were to continue with but few intermissions for a quarter of a century.

For her fame grew like the spread of a conflagration, and with much the same rapidity. Her services were sought in every capital. The crowned heads of the Continent one and all lavished applause and presents and distinctions upon her. Her father and brother-in-law escorted her everywhere, besides rigidly supervising her studies and guarding her against overwork, annoyance or climatic exposure. Even at this period (1862) Strakosch began to insist that she should be

---

[1] Her success there was extraordinary. At one concert the famous conductor gave her a message from a lady in the audience who had sent to tell him how much she had been struck by the beauty of her voice and her singing. Subsequently it transpired that the lady was no other than Jenny Lind.

spared the fatigue of rehearsing, except for operas that were new to her, and he frequently sang her parts at the ordinary *répétitions* in her stead. Her voice continued to grow; her unique timbre acquired an added richness, her *coloratura* a greater *maestria*, brilliancy, and precision. In her acting there was more life, more dramatic intelligence and feeling. Even her severest critic, Henry Chorley, found fewer faults to complain of.

When her lame sister Carlotta, now established in America as a concert soprano of remarkable talent, came to London (also under engagement to Mr Gye), no one thought of instituting comparisons. Carlotta could compete with the birds and display her amazing *bravura* at concerts if she pleased. But in opera, there was—there could be—but one *diva* and her name was Adelina! In a word the sisters did not get on well together; hence Carlotta did not form one of the family party when the younger girl went with her father and Maurice Strakosch to live at Rossini Villa, Clapham Park, which they made their home for some years.

Among their most frequent visitors there were Mario and Grisi, Balfe and his wife, Trebelli and Bettini, and Davison, the *Times* critic, with his wife, the celebrated pianist, Arabella Goddard. Her life, apart from her work, was that of most Victorian English girls. She had a German governess-chaperone Louise Lauwe, in addition to her lifelong companion, " Karo ", and assiduously cultivated her exceptional gift for foreign languages. She could converse equally well in English, French, Italian, and Spanish, with a smattering of Russian. She worked at her piano and improved her knowledge of music. She went out walking or driving and on "off-days" helped to entertain a few friends. She fell in love—and fell out again; suitors not being encouraged. She sang at Covent Garden one or twice a week—generally twice, never more; and never (except for a new opera) did she attend rehearsals. High-spirited and happy, she thoroughly enjoyed her existence. Somewhat below medium height, she was exceedingly elegant and pretty, had wonderful dark eyes, an expressive mouth with a delightful smile, a rich contralto *speaking* voice and a Southern temper that had no sooner burst out than it calmed down again.

Year after year she went abroad during the winter months, and fulfilled brilliant engagements in every European capital. As her triumphs grew, her terms rose, though as yet nowhere near the fabulous level they were to attain in the seventies and eighties. In every country she was received at Court and invested with decorations. Her great hit in 1863 was as Marguerite in Gounod's new opera *Faust*, which she sang first in Germany and afterwards in Spain and France, always, of course, in Italian. The city of her predilection was Paris. She loved being petted by the Parisians of the Second Empire and received at the Tuileries by the Emperor Napoleon and the Empress Eugénie. Unfortunately that Imperial intimacy was to prove her undoing—in a domestic sense. It was there she met the Emperor's equerry, the Marquis de Caux, and was persuaded by the Empress to accept him as her husband.

The wedding was celebrated at the Roman Catholic Church on Clapham Common on July 29th, 1868, and the Marquise stole only a brief holiday for her honeymoon. But the marriage proved an unhappy one.

After nine years the ill-matched couple agreed to separate. They were not finally divorced, however, until 1885 ; and long before then the singer had met and united her fortunes with those of her first " real love ", Ernest Nicolini, the well-known French tenor. She bought Craig-y-Nos Castle, in the Swansea Valley, and in 1886 became Adelina Patti-Nicolini, by which name she was known to her friends until her second husband's death in 1898. That space of twelve years was the happiest period of her life.

6

The pretty little theatre which she built at Craig-y-Nos Castle witnessed the ultimate evolution of her powers as an actress. The wordless plays in which she there took part constituted the sole medium through which, in her case, dramatic talent could continue to develop. For though she was still singing in public, both in England and abroad, and in 1895 returned to Covent Garden to make some final appearances in opera, her still-beautiful voice could now command only a limited range. Resistance to fatigue or strain was no longer to be incurred. And yet to the end her vocal art never retrograded.

During those interesting years I paid many visits to Craig-y-Nos. It was a remote out-of-the-way place (to-day converted into a Welsh hospital) and was a veritable fairy palace of luxury and recreation. Mme Patti-Nicolini and her husband made an ideal host and hostess. She had conceived a passion for miming in plays without speech or song, and it was extremely interesting to watch her in them. The mobility of her facial expression, the aptness and significance of her gestures, the litheness of her movements, her capacity for delineating character and portraying difficult scenes without uttering a sound—all these afforded new and striking evidence of her Italian origin. It was my privilege to arrange some of the wordless plays for her and even to act with her in them. Moreover, she still loved to sing; and the short scenes from operas and improvised concerts that would have cost her managers many hundreds of pounds were gladly offered without charge to her friends in the Swansea Valley.

One day at Craig-y-Nos Castle I asked Mme Patti to tell me which was her favourite rôle. She answered without a moment's hesitation that it was Rosina, then added, " I will tell you why : I like the *Barbiere* best of all my operas. I love the comedy and the constant fun. I can laugh and feel joyous all the time. Birds always sing best when they feel happy, *n'est-ce pas?* Besides, I revel in the ' Lesson Scene '. I can do just as I please there, and (now don't frown !) it always amuses me when I introduce music that was written years after Rossini wrote the opera. Yes, including ' Home, sweet Home '. I don't count that because it is like the extra bit of bread that the bakers used to give away with the loaf *quand j'étais une petite fille !* "

She was truly, in Hanslick's words, a born *comédienne* —almost as much so, in fact, as she was a born singer ; moreover, *très-musicale* without being *très-musicienne.* Her ear and memory were astonishing. Being a slow reader, she learned quickest by humming the music over as her *maestro al piano* played it. (Bevignani, her favourite conductor, told me this.) In certain familiar operas she knew every other part as well as her own. A strange tenor was once singing with her in *Rigoletto* somewhere in America, and the poor man was so nervous in the duet of the second act, that, at the point where he should have interrupted Gilda, he remained dumb. Instantly she took up his theme, singing, " T'amo, t'amo " to him where he should have sung it to her, and then resumed her own part. But the pretended student was so completely lost in mingled admiration and fright that he could not get a note out until the orchestra arrived at the well-known *andantino*. Then, like a recalcitrant motor-car, he managed to start his melody.

It has been said that Patti often sang music that was not worthy of her. It may be so. But we should not forget that, from her childhood onward, she had sung the old ballads with an unaffected simplicity that was in itself a joy and a delight. The public demanded these oft-heard favourites and would not be content unless she sang them. Few were aware, though, how frequently in her younger days she used to improvize the marvellous cadenzas that gushed like a torrent from her throat. That, of course, was long before the era of the so-called Patti Concerts. At the Albert Hall she never improvized the smallest change in " Une voce " or " Bel raggio ". Once she did contrive to puzzle her critics by adding a *coda* to Tosti's song " La Serenata " which was not to be found in the published copy. Yet somehow it sounded familiar, and I ultimately discovered that it belonged to a paraphrase of the song written and played by the violinist Simonetti. Patti had noticed it, liked it, and asked Tosti to transcribe it for her. But I never heard anyone else sing it.

7

There were as many sides to Adelina Patti's character and genius as there are facets to a brilliant, and each reflected a peculiar radiance of its own. Her life, like her artistry, presented different aspects with the childlike and spontaneous always uppermost. It was a pity in a way, that she should have been so acutely affected by her environment, or rather by the selfish dispositions and aims of the people around her. She changed as they came and went, and their contending influences were not invariably for the best. The one thing that never swerved from its perfection was the unsullied loveliness of her voice and her singing. As a woman, one might justly have applied to her the French saying, *Souvent femme varie.* Her variations, however, were not as a rule due to mere mood or caprice, to unstable temperament or fundamental faults of character. They were slow to develop because in the main her nature was a deeply-rooted one, and, had its finer qualities been strong enough to offer a sturdier resistance, probably there would have been fewer changes to note—and deplore.

As it was, what has been designated " The Reign of Patti " might be divided into Five Ages : at first the prodigy ; the fascinating child and miraculous little singer. The second the youthful prima donna ; with easy triumphs and dreams of still greater to come ; a springtide radiant with irresponsible happiness and secret hopes for a romantic future. The third or " Marquise " period, the age of glorious artistic successes and universal adoration ; likewise of secret disappointment and *désillusionement.* (It was then that her nature grew harder, less trustful, slightly

suspicious even.) The fourth or " Nicolini " period
was the " time of roses ", the brief span of joyous
companionship and home-life, combined with sys-
tematic fortune-earning, constant travel and hard
work; the " Queen of Song " surrounded by her
courtiers, bountiful with her gifts and more inclined
than before to be generous in the cause of charity.

The fifth, or " last scene of all ", covered a space of
twenty years; that is to say, from her marriage in
1899 with Baron Rolf Cederström until her death on
September 27th, 1919. The age of romance was past;
she was nearly 56 on the date of her third wedding.
Her new husband was a Swedish doctor in his thirties,
and she believed herself to be in love yet once again.
Quickly and surely her outlook on life underwent a
final change and, with but few exceptions, her old
friends became completely separated from her. Her
health deteriorated, the robust constitution that had
enabled her to lead a laborious life from the age of
seven began at last to weaken and give way. Craig-y-
Nos Castle saw no more fêtes, no more theatricals,
very little music, no gaiety whatsoever. In 1903 she
visited America for a final farewell tour. On October
20, 1914, she made her last appearance in public (then
in her 72nd year) at a concert given at the Albert Hall
in aid of the Red Cross War Fund. There for the last
time we heard her sing " Home, sweet Home " in her
own unforgettable manner and with all the magical
charm of old.

When she divorced the Marquis de Caux, she handed
to him half her fortune—a large sum; but the loss
must have been speedily recouped. Her terms had
long been higher than any other singer's, even so far
back as the seventies, when Gye paid her only 200

guineas a night. But for years Percy Harrison, her concert impresario, paid her 800 guineas every time she appeared at the Albert Hall and 600 guineas for every concert in the provinces. In the States she received £1000 or £1200 for each operatic performance, and in the Argentine still higher sums ; while on her farewell concert tour in North America it was officially stated that she netted £50,000. She was, therefore, a very rich woman. Her career of fifty-six years as a public performer was without parallel either for length or for brilliancy. Taken for all in all, she was by far the most wonderful singer of her time.

She died at Craig-y-Nos Castle and was interred at Père la Chaise Cemetery, Paris, after the remains had been deposited for a night en route at the Kensal Green Cemetery, where Tietjens lay buried and where a service was held in the presence of a few old friends. Her vast fortune was inherited by Baron Cederström and transferred by him to his native land. He also took away to Stockholm all her wonderful stage costumes, her operatic scores, etc., to be placed in the Museum there, but gave scarcely a souvenir to any of her former friends in England. What ultimately became of her magnificent jewels, worth hundreds of thousands of pounds, was never disclosed.

CHAPTER IV

PAULINE LUCCA

AND HER RENOWNED RIVALS

I

IT was something of a coincidence that one short
mid-Victorian decade should have witnessed the keen
rivalry existing between four of the greatest sopranos
that ever sang in London. They were first appearing
here at one time—Tietjens, Patti, Lucca, and Nilsson—
in 1867, the season in which the Swedish artist made
her début at Her Majesty's. The same brilliant
quartet reassembled pretty regularly 1877, until when
the much-loved Tietjens disappeared from the scene.
Patti, who came in 1861, only preceded Pauline Lucca
by two years, so that the entire constellation spread
its effulgence over our local firmament within a space
of nine seasons.

That the effort of one star to outshine another bred
jealousies is not to be gainsaid. The four were well
" at it ", indeed, what time the present writer began
edging his way into the gallery at Covent Garden and
Her Majesty's. But even before then he had been
listening to lively arguments over the family tea-table
about the relative merits of these distinguished *prime
donne ;* to discussions as to how supreme each was in
her particular line ; how each had her own special

PAULINE LUCCA

rôle or group of rôles wherein the others could not approach her. All went well, I concluded, so long as they steered clear of each other's particular domain. And that they generally succeeded in doing except in the matter of one alluring part, to wit, Marguerite in Gounod's *Faust*.

The new opera had come over fresh from Paris in Pauline Lucca's first year here—1863 ; but that season the part of the heroine was only sung by Tietjens at Her Majesty's and by Miolan-Carvalho (the original French Marguerite) at Covent Garden. In the following year it was undertaken at Covent Garden both by Pauline Lucca and Adelina Patti ; and three years later not only by them but by Christine Nilsson. Then began the invidious game of comparisons. It was unanimously agreed that Tietjens did not look the part ; she was too stout and not dreamy enough. Patti was open to criticism because she did not act it with sufficient passion, though she sang the music divinely.

Lucca, however, did both, for she sang and acted splendidly ; but her Marguerite was considered a " very forward minx ", and " a titter always went round the house when the curtain fell upon the Garden Scene ". (By the way, it was actually questioned at the time whether this episode was altogether " proper ", and whether the opera ought to have been licensed by the Lord Chamberlain.) Regarding Nilsson's Marguerite one heard nought save undiluted praise. It was pronounced to be in every respect absolutely ideal ; and after all these years I again venture to declare that to be my own opinion too.

It has been worth while to recall these burning rivalries of the sixties, not only because they were

replete with absorbing interest to the opera-goers of
that period, but because they indicate more clearly
the class of talent, the strength of the opposing forces
that a newcomer had then to contend against, compared with the easy task that would await, let us say, a
Pauline Lucca to-day. She, as we are about to see, was
a genius fully as remarkable in her way as any of the
famous singers whom she encountered upon the
terrain of Italian Opera. Only she was a trifle unlucky
to have had to struggle in the same arena against
three giants who were practically as big as herself. As
it was, she proved strong enough to hold her own, and,
indeed, instead of suffering by comparison with them,
she left behind a reputation so high that the present
generation may be glad to hear more about her.

One point should be remembered. Pauline Lucca
did not take part in the historic " Coalition season " of
1869, when, Her Majesty's Theatre having been
reduced to ashes, Gye and Mapleson joined forces in
Bow Street. Whether it was because she declined to
enter the lists against her illustrious antagonists at
close quarters was never made clear; anyhow she
refused to come. And, if she had, the problem would
have been even harder for the two impresarios than
that which faced Benjamin Lumley at Her Majesty's in
1845, when he had in his company four of the most
celebrated ballet-dancers of the century—Taglioni,
Carlotta Grisi, Cerito, and Lucille Grahn (Fanny
Elssler was *not* one of the quartet as has often been
stated).

Lumley got out of his difficulty by devising the
famous " Pas de Quatre ", wherein the great *ballerines*
could all display their consummate gifts simultaneously
—or nearly so—once the question of the order of

their appearance had been settled.[1]   But it is easier to arrange these matters in a ballet than in an opera.   The outstanding achievement of 1869 was the all-star cast of *Don Giovanni*.   There would have been no room in that combination for Pauline Lucca ; and in any other Mozart opera of the ordinary repertory one of the four *prime donne* must equally have been left out.

2

" One of the most brilliant operatic artists of a brilliant epoch ", Pauline Lucca was born of Italian parents at Vienna on April 25, 1841.   Her unusually strong " girl's voice " attracted notice, and several teachers in the town took her in hand.   But pecuniary means were lacking for more advanced study until one day she acted as *remplaçante* for the soprano soloist at the Karl-Kirche, where she was singing in the choir.   Then some leading musical notabilities,

---

[1] Lumley has related in his *Reminiscences of the Opera* how the solution was arrived at : " The place of honour, the last in such cases (as in regal processions), had been ceded without overmuch hesitation to Mademoiselle Taglioni. Of the remaining ladies who claimed equal rights, founded on talent and popularity, neither would appear before the other. ' *Mon Dieu !* ' exclaimed the ballet-master in distress, ' *Cerito ne veut pas commencer avant Carolotta—ni Carlotta avant Cerito, et il n'y a pas moyen de les faire bouger ; tout est fini !* ' . . . Said I,—' Let the *oldest* take her unquestionable right to the envied position ! ' The ballet-master smote his forehead, smiled assent, and bounded from the room upon the stage. The judgment of the manager was announced. The ladies tittered, laughed, drew back, and were now as much disinclined to accept the right of position as they had before been eager to claim it. The ruse succeeded ".   The " Pas de Quatre " was the talk of London for years.

perceiving her exceptional talent, arranged to defray the cost of her vocal training, first under Richard Levy, and later under Otto Uffmann. To obtain stage experience, she also entered the chorus of the Hofoper and soon made her mark in the small part of the chief bridesmaid in *Der Freischütz*. This led to her being engaged to sing Italian parts at the opera-house at Olmütz, where she made her début in September, 1859, as Elvira in Verdi's *Ernani*, and achieved an instantaneous success.

But Olmütz was not to keep her for long. Prague had heard of her and offered her a contract. She was on the point of leaving for the Bohemian capital when something unpleasant happened. One of her fair companions in the company, jealous of her success, took occasion at rehearsal to insult her rather grossly. Pauline went straight to the manager and told him that unless she received an ample apology she would never come back to sing at Olmütz again. His reply took the form of a threat to have her imprisoned unless she completed her contract. That was enough for the high-spirited Pauline.

Determined not to give way or to let the manager get the benefit of her services, she walked off to the citadel and gave herself up as an offender against the law. She slept that night in a detention-cell. On the following day the hubbub caused in the town by her conduct aroused the hoped-for popular indignation, and in consequence the artist who had started the trouble was compelled to apologize. Thereupon Fräulein Lucca left forthwith for Prague, where, in March, 1860, she made a second successful début, this time as Valentine in *Les Huguenots*.

We arrive here at the first important turning-point

in the career of a singer who was almost as famous for her wilful and capricious temper as for her fascinating and all-conquering genius. Unfortunately, little first-hand information is available concerning the details of her early essays in opera; but when the simple facts are as picturesque as they were in her case, the ordinary minutiæ of artistic development do not matter much. Besides, a comparatively short time was to elapse before Lucca made her first appearance in London, and our chief interest in the woman and her art really dates from that event.

What occurred then, at Prague? To begin with, we find our youthful prima donna of 19 suddenly cutting adrift from her Olmütz répertoire of *soprano leggiero* parts, such as Elvira in *Ernani*, and—like Patti at New Orleans in the very same year—shouldering the dramatic soprano burden of Valentine in *Les Huguenots*. Not alone that. It is on record that now and then in Prague she sang Norma—another heavy rôle, even if not essentially designed for stout ladies in particular, as was formerly inferred from the fact that it was Tietjens's own *cheval de bataille*.

Anyhow, the name of Pauline Lucca was on all lips when one day the mighty Intendant of the Royal Theatre and Opera-House at Berlin, Baron von Hülsen, found himself by chance in the ancient city of Prague. Naturally he went to hear the new Valentine; and the experience is said to have deprived him of the power of speech for every purpose save that of securing this gifted creature for his own capital. Needless to say the Baron succeeded. He signed a contract with her for the following season for more thalers per month than he had ever before paid to a *débutante*; which contract was destined to be supplemented soon

afterwards by a decree that made the young lady
" Court-singer to the King of Prussia " for life.

I have found no confirmation of the statement that
Pauline Lucca was engaged for Berlin through the
influence of Meyerbeer; or even that he asked the
Baron von Hülsen to go to Prague to hear her. What
we do know for certain is that at that period Meyerbeer
was living in Berlin and working on his last opera,
L'Africaine; that he was on the look-out for a singer
to create the part of the dusky heroine; and furthermore, that it was after he had witnessed Lucca's
glorious performance of Valentine at Berlin—*i.e.* the
first time he ever saw her—that he was heard to
exclaim, " There is my Selika ! "

When her parents learned the news at Vienna it
caused them mingled joy and regret: joy that their
little girl should have been " born under such a lucky
star ", and regret because it was unlikely that either
Berlin or Meyerbeer would tolerate for the present the
idea of letting her return to her native town. As a
matter of fact, she accepted Meyerbeer's offer instantly
and with unfeigned delight. Without loss of time she
began to study the rôle of Selika with the composer,
although the new opera was not yet nearly completed.

3

It would be difficult to furnish an adequate picture
of the sensation that Pauline Lucca aroused during her
first season in Berlin. Her début, be it noted, took
place on April 1, 1861, just six weeks prior to the first
appearance of Patti at Covent Garden. That event it
strongly resembled, both in regard to the nature and
extent of the local enthusiasm and its repercussion in

the opera-houses of Germany and Austria. The rush to hear her increased each time her name appeared in the bills. The announcement, " Lucca is singing to-night ", sufficed to crowd the big house from floor to ceiling.

Her dramatic talent is said to have taken on an added subtlety and power with each fresh character that she portrayed. Her voice must have been entrancingly beautiful in the dawn of its freshness, seeing how wonderfully rich and matured it sounded to my ears ten years later. It aroused the ecstatic admiration of the Berlin critics though they had perforce to admit that her vocal technique still left much to be desired. For her *coloratura*, if fluent and crisp, was neither brilliant nor dazzling. It had not come to her " naturally ", with little or no instruction, as, for example, Patti's had come to her whilst she was still in her teens.[1]

---

[1] An interesting comparison between Patti and Lucca is drawn by the late Mathilde Marchesi in her book, *Marchesi and Music*. It may appropriately be quoted here, although it refers to a later period (1876), when the two stars were shining simultaneously at the Italian Opera in Vienna. Says the famous teacher :

" This was a rare treat, for every evening one had the choice between Patti, with her extraordinarily beautiful voice and delightful method, and Lucca with her marvellous dramatic talent. The former excited the greatest admiration and carried us quite away with the charm of her singing ; but the latter appealed to the feelings of her audiences and in great dramatic moments would take our hearts by storm. It was a thousand pities that Lucca's natural and remarkable talent should not have been properly cultivated. The wonderful progress she subsequently made in her singing was mainly due to the excellent example of Italian singers she had before her ; she was the best Carmen I ever saw ".

Enough has been said to show that Pauline's success in Berlin was something quite out of the common. Her versatility astounded the *cognoscenti*. After realizing the tragic grandeur of her Norma, her Agathe, her Leonora and her Valentine, they loved to revel in the irresistible comedy of her two great juvenile impersonations, Cherubino in *Figaro* and Zerlina in *Fra Diavolo*, which she thenceforward made her own. No wonder Meyerbeer saw in her his ideal Selika. He became more and more anxious that she should be the first artist to undertake the part.

Unluckily, that was not to be. *L'Africaine* had been promised by Meyerbeer to the Paris Opéra, and there it would have to be sung to the French text of its author, Eugène Scribe. The latter had originally handed it to the composer so long before as 1840 (together with that of *Le Prophète*) and again in its ultimate revised form in 1852. The authorities were quite willing to engage any special artist selected by Meyerbeer; but Lucca, greatly though she appreciated the honour, positively declined to accept it. She had never sung in French; she did not care to learn; and nothing should induce her to undertake either the trouble or the responsibility of such a task. Someone else, for aught she cared, might be the Selika in Paris; she "would afterwards create the part elsewhere". And, as we shall see, that was what actually came to pass.

4

Towards the close of that phenomenal year, 1861, whilst Pauline Lucca was living and studying in Berlin, she received a surprise visit from no less a person than Adelina Patti. The two young women had never seen

each other. Until the preceding spring both had been
practically unknown to the larger European public.
But, after her amazing triumph in London, the new
diva had been engaged through her brother-in-law,
Maurice Strakosch, for a few " guest " performances
at the Berlin Hofoper during the month of December.
At that moment Pauline was not singing; but
Strakosch, always well informed on operatic matters,
had heard of her vogue in the Prussian capital, and
determined to take his little relative to see her in her
" modest lodgings ". He says in his amusing book,
Souvenirs d'un Impresario : " They found her in bed,
looking very juvenile and interesting. Her first word
was an exclamation of surprise on beholding Adelina
Patti—herself a sweet and adorable creature. ' What ! '
exclaimed Lucca, almost involuntarily, ' can *you* be the
great Patti ? ' " Instead of telling us what followed
he merely adds that, " The rivalry between the
two singers existed only upon the stage, for outside the theatre they were always upon the best
terms of *camaraderie* ". Which I venture rather to
doubt.

Only another year at Berlin—all idea of persuading
Pauline to go to Paris being finally abandoned—and
one fine spring morning, on entering Meyerbeer's
study, her beloved master and friend greets her with
the news that he has been entrusted by Mr Frederic
Gye with an offer for her to sing in London during the
current season (1863). With a cry of joy, she rushes
forward to embrace him, accepts the offer, and signs
the contract without even troubling to look at the
terms. This incident is worth recalling, as a preliminary to her first journey to London, inasmuch as
she made the terms in question the ostensible ground

for an entirely novel and eccentric line of behaviour during her stay in England.

In what still remained of the season of 1863 there was little time for anything beyond the actual début, which took place on July 18th. It was an exceptionally brilliant success. Covent Garden, filled to overflowing, rapturously welcomed Pauline Lucca in her superb assumption of Valentine in *Les Huguenots*. The critics were unanimous in their praise. Considerably below medium height, she struck them as rather short in stature for the part; but this disadvantage did not prevent her from asserting in full measure the irresistible, the almost uncanny power of the passionate intensity and feeling that imbued her singing and acting. Her dark-complexioned oval face, her lustrous eyes, her oriental type of beauty, combined with a singular variety of facial expression, lent her an extraordinary physical attractiveness. Her significant gestures and graceful, panther-like tread made her immensely interesting to watch.

This rare quality of sensuous charm was abundantly reflected in a voice of wonderful purity and sweetness. It resembled in a peculiar degree the clear, rich, penetrating timbre of a clarinet, with a touching human quality replacing the " reedy " timbre of the woodwind instrument. Its mellowness gave it a direct emotional appeal which awakened a responsive chord in the heart as well as the ear; for it owed far more to nature than to art. The scale was even and smooth throughout a range extending easily to the D in *alt*. She possessed admirable breath-control and adequate though by no means extraordinary flexibility of *bravura* execution. In 1863 certain points in Lucca's technique were undoubtedly open to criticism; and

Chorley and Davison knew how to analyze them. Ten years later, when the present writer was beginning to hear her in all her famous parts, the loopholes had either disappeared or were not to be perceived in the delight of enjoying the sheer beauty of her performance.

5

In 1864 came a notorious *reprise* of *Faust* (newly mounted at Covent Garden during the preceding season) with Pauline Lucca for the first time as Marguerite. Mario took the title-rôle and Faure his original character of Mephistopheles. It made a sensation—as well it might; yet not entirely of the kind that had been anticipated. There was, in the opinion of the critics, a " fly in the ointment ". They would not accept as correct or becoming Mlle Lucca's reading of the Garden Scene. She was altogether too coquettish, too " flirtatious ", or, as one writer gracefully put it, " far too ' *knowing* ' to have captivated so refined and gentlemanly a Faust as Signor Mario ! " Mr Gye, though sympathetic, suggested that, in order to placate the critics and prevent possible trouble with the Lord Chamberlain (*sic*) it might be advisable for the " forward Margherita " to modify some of her business.

The young lady refused, however, to do anything of the sort. She declared that she knew a great deal more about the character of the German Gretchen than did either French artists or English critics. She would act the part in her way or not at all. Thoroughly annoyed, she took umbrage at the attitude of everybody, both inside and outside the opera-house, and insisted that there was a conspiracy to injure her reputation. Furthermore, she declined to remain any longer " in a town where such things were possible ". Accordingly, early in the month of June, she pleaded ill-health and took her departure for Berlin, " leaving her manager in the lurch and, to all appearance, shaking the dust of London from her shoes for ever ".

Rumour credited the temperamental Pauline with other reasons for leaving—among them the fogs that arose from our " muddy river " Thames, mingling with the smell of decaying vegetables from Covent Garden market ; but the real cause, of course, was the *Faust* affair. It had happened at a moment when she was dissatisfied with her salary here and genuinely upset by the death of Meyerbeer, which had occurred only a month before.

Whilst she was singing subsequently at Berlin and Vienna preparations were going on in Paris for the long-deferred production of *L'Africaine*. That event ultimately took place on April 28, 1865, Marie Sasse being the Selika, Naudin the Vasco da Gama, and Faure the Nelusko. The new opera enjoyed an enormous vogue, and this quickly had a bearing upon the forgiving spirit of Mr Gye. That astute manager, who had threatened his wayward prima donna with fines and imprisonment if she ever gave him the chance, withdrew his legal proceedings and, after due negotiation, re-engaged her for the current season to " create " Selika in his forthcoming Italian production of *L'Africaine* at Covent Garden.

Then it was that Pauline Lucca really came, saw, and conquered. As one writer said, " her impersonation of Selika must be ranked among the very highest achievements in the lyric drama ". One can only add, what a pity that Meyerbeer should not have lived to hear his " swan song " or to behold the Selika of his dreams! And it was also to be regretted that the latter, thanks to the red-tape laws of the Paris Opéra, should never have been seen upon the boards where *L'Africaine*, a quarter of a century later, attained a total of 500 representations.

During each of the many seasons that she continued to appear at Covent Garden, Pauline Lucca never failed to make half a dozen appearances in her favourite rôle. In 1868, for instance, when she was singing with Mario in *Les Huguenots*, *La Favorita*, and *Faust*, when the quaint, boyish humour of her Cherubino and the no less girlish grace and charm of her Zerlina in *Fra Diavolo* were delighting opera-goers, it was still her glorious Selika that carried off the palm. Four years later I was lucky enough to hear her in the part myself, with Naudin and Faure in their original characters ; and that experience, it need scarcely be said, remains deeply imprinted on my memory.

What a picture she made as the swarthy, amorous African Queen! What an entrance!—the barbaric dignity of it,—the slowness of her gliding motion when she follows Vasco da Gama into the Admiralty Hall at Lisbon with Nelusko at her heels, he crouching and full of menace! Her glance seemed to magnetize the whole assemblage, both on the stage and in the auditorium. Then the contrast of the succeeding scene in the prison where Vasco lies sleeping ; the soothing silkiness of Selika's *berceuse*, alternating with her outbursts of passionate devotion and apprehension. Here we listened to a gorgeous voice and exquisite singing. The whirlwind changes in the last two acts from one extreme to another of adoration and anger rendered the spectator literally breathless ; and the climax came with the tragic ending beneath the deadly branches of the upas-tree. I have seen many Selikas (including Gabrielle Krauss's fine performance with Lassalle at Paris in 1879); but Pauline Lucca's left them all far behind alike in nobility of conception and savage grandeur.

6

She did not return to England after the season of 1872 for ten years. During the interval she was heard in the principal opera-houses of Germany, Austria, and Russia; and she also made a two years' stay in America, adding constantly to a repertory that eventually comprised over fifty rôles. She had in 1869 married Baron von Rhaden and, after her separation from him in '72, Baron von Wallhofen. The latter name she bore in private when I was introduced to her during her last visit to London in 1884. I found her an amiable and vivacious personage, and we became very good friends. Besides retaining all her beauty (she was still only 43), " her voice had lost none of its freshness, and the piquant grace of her style and the marked originality of her conceptions were even more striking than before ".[1]

London delighted once again in her incomparable Selika and many of the former favourites of her repertory. But her Carmen was new, and, as it turned out, worth placing well in the forefront of the collection. It struck a happy mean between the positively broad or vulgar and the over-refined; being in this respect more highly-coloured than the Carmens of Galli-Marié (the original) or Minnie Hauk, more

[1] *Thirty Years of Musical Life in London* (p. 158).

Viennese and less definitely Spanish than those of
Calvé and Zélie de Lussan. In any case, Lucca's was
equal to the finest of them in "all the attributes of
voluptuous charm, subtle power and dramatic intensity that the character demands "; while her rendering
of Bizet's wonderful music has never, perhaps, been
equalled for picturesque beauty and force.

She was rather fond of practical jokes—mostly of a
mild, harmless description. It was by semi-jocular
tricks that she persuaded Bismarck to allow himself to
be photographed with her (the photo was sold all over
the Continent for years), and to grant her a special
pass to visit the German army front in the War of
1870–1. Her curious adventures near Metz aroused
considerable curiosity at the time.

Pauline Lucca's final home was in her birthplace,
Vienna. She had settled down there after her return
from America in 1874, and continued to sing in opera
for many years before retiring from the stage and
devoting herself to teaching. She died in 1908.

F

CHAPTER V

CHRISTINE NILSSON

THE SECOND "SWEDISH NIGHTINGALE"

I

THEY were fond of distinguishing their favourites by *sobriquets* in the operatic world of the Victorian age. Even as Patti inherited the title of *Diva*, so, not long afterwards, did Christine Nilsson succeed to that of " The Swedish Nightingale ", created for Jenny Lind. The exact difference in current value between the two distinctions it would have been hard to assay. At this date one point alone is clear : the matter was one with which nationality had something to do. A *diva* ought, properly speaking, to be of Italian birth or descent, yet might conceivably be a native of any country ; whereas in the case of a " Swedish Nightingale " it is a primary condition that she should be a Swede. And that Christine Nilsson undoubtedly was.

A dreamy, poetic, sylph-like creature ; tall and graceful ; with a marvellous complexion, clear, blue-grey eyes, a pretty mouth and markedly Scandinavian features, her beauty and her voice were both at their fullest perfection when I first heard her during George Wood's Italian season at Drury Lane in 1870. It was only her fourth summer in London, and she was a month or so short of twenty-seven. As chance would

CHRISTINE NILSSON

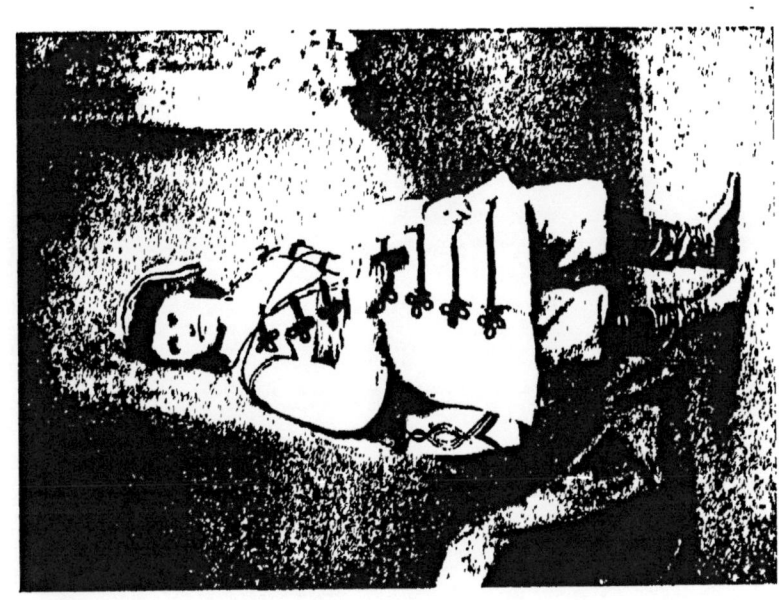

NILSSON AS MIGNON

have it, George Wood's artists—" borrowed " by him from Her Majesty's Theatre, which at that time was closed—were giving *Roberto il Diavolo* at Drury Lane with a remarkable cast, including Mongini (Roberto), Gardoni (Rambaldo), Foli (Bertramo), Ilma di Murska (Isabella), and Christine Nilsson (Alice) ; Arditi being the conductor. My parents, ardent admirers of Meyerbeer, were unable to resist the temptation of going to hear this performance of a now half-forgotten opera, and, by great good luck, they decided to take with them their eldest son, then a musical fanatic of fourteen.

Alice was considered to be one of Christine Nilsson's best rôles, and I was always glad to have seen her in it before making acquaintance with her yet more famous Marguerite. The types were somewhat analogous, despite their different nationalities. The Norman peasant girl, with her braided flaxen locks, might have been first cousin to the German Gretchen ; and both were exquisitely fair in the person of Christine Nilsson, then only just in the bloom of womanhood.

I see her now, wearing her plain short frock, coming upon the scene in search of her foster-brother, Robert of Normandy. The rapt expression in her steely eyes told of the maiden's resolute spirit as she warbled in a voice of incredible sweetness her quaint romance, " Nel lasciar la Normandia ". Her fight against the powers of evil that night was to dwell in my memory as the foreshadowing of her struggle in the prison scene of Gounod's opera. In both she attained the perfect ideal. Her Alice was the embodiment of spiritual strength ; her Marguerite the acme of womanly charm. There was about each a measure of poetry and romance, an ethereal quality, that lifted the character clean out of the ordinary atmosphere of the world and daily life.

It was this same ethereal quality, as I was to find in after years, that also lent such extraordinary individuality and attractiveness to Nilsson's impersonations of Ophelia (created by her in Paris), of Mignon (first time in England at Drury Lane in 1870), of Elsa, of Desdemona (Rossini's), and other of her poetic characters. At the same time she had the rare dramatic power that sufficed, together with superb singing, to make her Donna Elvira and Queen of Night not a whit less satisfying. In all of these varied rôles it was my good fortune to hear her at the height of her powers. I heard her also as Valentine in *Les Huguenots* and Leonora in *Il Trovatore*, but in them admired her less. With the purely vocal side of her genius I will deal later. First let me say something about the strange history of her earlier days.

2

Christine Nilsson was the seventh child of a seventh child. She was born in a forest hut near Wexio, in Sweden, on August 20th, 1843, the same year as that which saw the birth of Adelina Patti. Her parents were struggling peasants; one of her brothers an itinerant violinist, who taught her his instrument.[1]

[1] " We wandered through the streets of our native town ", she once related to a friend, " displaying our talents and bringing the money we earned home to our parents. Whenever our mother saw a stranger approach our place, she drove us out into the street, and we were forced to persecute the new-comer with our performance until, to get rid of us, he bestowed something upon us ".

She showed precocious musical talent, and one day, at a neighbouring fair, attracted the attention of a local magistrate, who adopted her. Finding that she had a voice of more than ordinary promise, another friend, the Baroness Lurhusen, herself a well-known singer, gave her lessons, and she made rapid progress. At the age of 15 she was sent by her guardian to Stockholm to study under Franz Berwald, and worked during the same period at her violin.

Indeed, at a benefit concert given for her in the capital she played a violin concerto in addition to singing an air from *Robert le Diable*. Thence she went, with Baroness Lurhusen, to Paris, to take finishing lessons, and was accepted as a pupil by Pierre Wartel—an *ancien ténor* of the Opéra and the teacher of Trebelli. In his capable hands she developed into the artist who was to take the French capital by storm. Engaged by Carvalho for the Théâtre-Lyrique, she there made her début at the age of 21, on October 27th, 1864, as the heroine of a new French version of *La Traviata*.

Like Piccolomini and Patti before her, the Swedish soprano proved gifted enough to overcome the dislike of the Parisians for an opera which they always declared to be *trop triste*, "above all at the end, where a dying woman *will* insist on singing instead of going to bed". In a word, they preferred Dumas *fils* and Aimée Desclée to Verdi and his "noisy accompaniments". But in spite of that, the new Violetta made a highly favourable impression and quickly followed it up with an even bigger hit as the Queen of Night in *The Magic Flute*. One prominent French critic wrote: "Like a true daughter of the North, like a sister of Jenny Lind, Christine Nilsson has entered into the master's idea. If her clear and resonant voice scales the heavens, it is to curse from on high like a daughter of the Titans. The notes spring from her mouth like fiery serpents. She has the laugh-rattle of a Hecate". Such was the Parisian concept of Astrifiammante.

In 1867 Mapleson saw in Christine Nilsson a possible rival to Patti. He engaged her on reasonable terms for Her Majesty's Theatre, where she made her début on June 8th as Violetta. She won a triumphant success, creating a sensation that all but realized her manager's expectations, and filling the house every night she sang. Not that Society thought of neglecting its admired *diva*; far from it. There were separate groups of subscribers at each of the London opera-houses, and not a few wealthy enthusiasts who supported both. So it became the fashion to go to hear Patti and Nilsson on alternate nights and relish the enjoyment of comparing them in the same rôles.

The new " Swedish Nightingale ", as she had been promptly named, was not the kind of person to quail before this ordeal. On the contrary, greatly daring, she rather invited comparisons by singing Patti's favourite parts ; and not alone hers but some of those associated with Tietjens, who was in the same troupe with herself. Thus, after her Violetta, she drove the nail home with her unapproachable Marguerite and her two other Paris hits, Martha and Donna Elvira. The latter—a revelation of pure Mozart singing in that particular part for the generation that heard it—gained much by juxtaposition with the glorious Donna Anna of Tietjens.

3

Apart from the effect of Nilsson's extraordinary personal beauty and poetic charm, the predominant impression she created both as singer and actress was one of astonishing originality. There was about her singing a quality that suggested the idea of a supernatural musical being of the type of fairies or water-nymphs or Rhinemaidens. It struck one most of all, perhaps, in the curious bell-like ring of a voice that was sweetly metallic and deliciously pure; that had a seductive timbre such as the " Loreley " might have simulated, only more human and emotional in its appeal and intensely musical throughout. Whilst generally cold and without passion, it seemed to derive a glow of warmth from the singer's method of phrasing and more particularly her art of modulating it with a delicately-graduated swell or *messa di voce*. This purely Italian gift she had acquired (when I heard her) not only from her teacher Wartel but from the gifted director of her later studies, Manuel Garcia.

With reference to her unique timbre, the following observation is made by Wm Kuhe in his *Reminiscences* : ". . . But a beautiful voice, too—a voice of extraordinary flexibility, richness, purity and, more than this, of remarkable individuality. It was always this peculiar timbre that I considered the diva's (*sic*) principal attraction. Had I, after a number of years, and blindfolded, heard her again, I should, by reason of this individuality of voice have exclaimed at once, ' That must be Nilsson ! ' " The same authority goes on to speak of her acting, about which there was " nothing conventional " ; for it was, truly, " wholly original ". Yet Mr Kuhe did not care for her Violetta so much as for Patti's; and I agree with him. Nilsson's was a novel treatment of the part, just as she gave us fresh readings of Elsa, Lucia, Marguerite (both Gounod's and Boito's), and Mignon. She did not invite comparisons by the common device of inventing new " business ", but simply allowed her imagination and dramatic resources free play. She made her points from opportunities that grew naturally out of the scene, with the result that on the stage she was always profoundly interesting. I only saw her once in an entirely new part. In Paris she created two, viz., Myrrha in *Sardanapale*, and Estelle in *Les Bluëts;* but here her sole creation was Edith Plantagenet, at Her Majesty's (June, 1874) in Balfe's melodious Italian Opera, *Il Talismano.* It struck me, I recollect, that she made impressive and sympathetic a character which in other hands might have been very dull and ordinary.

Like most prima donnas who were blessed with original ideas and a highly-strung artistic temperament, she was a somewhat difficult woman to deal with. If Patti had the wilfulness of a spoilt child, Nilsson possessed the stubbornness of an obstinate woman. Mapleson more than once discovered this to his cost; and it came the harder to him because he had long had for his mainstay a " comparative angel " in Theresa Tietjens, who was constantly arguing with him upon the futility of not giving way to Nilsson.

When the latter heard that Patti was getting £200 a night at Covent Garden she insisted on being paid the same amount; and Mapleson had no alternative but to consent. On hearing this, Patti (or was it her brother-in-law, Strakosch?) refused to sing for the same *cachet* that Nilsson received. When, however, Gye compromised by making her an offer of 200 *guineas*, Patti withdrew her objection. In spite of her stubborn nature, however, the capricious Christine had a kind heart. She combined much quiet generosity with her habit of profiting to the utmost by her undoubted drawing power—as, indeed, was her right. She never forgot her needy family in Sweden, but regularly sent them substantial sums. Moreover, she never broke a promise to perform a kind action.

In this way she once risked giving mortal offence to Queen Victoria. She was summoned to Windsor Castle on a day when she had undertaken to sing for poor girls at a convent near London. The " Master of the Musick " (Sir Wm Cusins) returned to the Castle in fear and trepidation with the message that Mlle Nilsson was unable to obey the Queen's command. But as soon as the Queen learned the reason, the royal frown disappeared and Her Majesty sent for another singer. Nilsson was, nevertheless, duly invited for the next available date, and, after she had sung, received at the Royal hands not only compliments, but a valuable bracelet of rubies and diamonds.

Once, early in the eighties, she travelled a long distance to appear at a concert at St. James's Hall, in aid of the Westminster Maternity Charity; and on that occasion I heard her sing for the first time Arthur Sullivan's ballad, " Let me dream again ", accompanied at the piano by the composer. Similarly, in 1891, four years after her retirement (being then the Countess Casa de Miranda), she came all the way from Madrid expressly to fulfil a promise she had made to Sims Reeves that she would take part in his farewell concert at the Royal Albert Hall. They sang together the duet, " Parigi, o cara ", from *La Traviata*.

She was not, strictly speaking, a *soprano leggiero* (or, as one would now term it, a *coloratura* singer), though in the early part of her career her voice extended over nearly three octaves, from G (below middle C) to the F in *alt*. But Rossini, when he heard her in Paris as the Queen of Night, advised her not to go as a rule above the high D. She took his advice, except in *tours de force* like the mad scenes of *Hamlet* and *Lucia*, in both of which I heard her touch the E in *alt*. However, as she grew older and stouter, her voice refused her these luxuries, whilst acquiring in its purely " dramatic " range a degree of opulence and power which it never lost so long as she remained a public singer.

Her agility in the airs of Donna Elvira, Lucia, Violetta, and Leonora was remarkable for its sustained brilliancy, ease, and precision. I have never forgotten, apart from that haunting singularity of her tone, the rare elegance of her execution in the more showy passages of Verdi. I may quote on this point the evidence of her conductor, Luigi Arditi, writing about her début in *La Traviata* :

" Nilsson's singing reminded me greatly of Angiolina Bosio, her brilliant *fioriture* being delivered with the same exquisite grace and refinement that characterized the style of the Italian artist. Everything was in favour of the young Swedish artist ; her youthful freshness—in itself a priceless charm—a definite individuality, her slight, supple figure, which lent itself to the draping of any classical robe, and above all the voice, of extensive compass, mellow, sweet, and rich ".

4

In the absence of temperamental warmth or passion, it was wonderful how in certain music she had the power of moving her audiences as she did. Naturally in a part like Elsa there was nothing surprising about that. Her very coldness seemed to account for the fact that in Wagner's heroine curiosity got the better of discretion. On the other hand, the same lack of spontaneous impulse, allied to the impeccable purity of her tone, intonation and style, fully explained her success in oratorio, which was for a time second only to that of Tietjens. Like Patti, she sang at a Birmingham Festival during her first season in this country, while in the following year she achieved an even more notable triumph at the Handel Festival. After that she appeared regularly with the Sacred Harmonic Society under Costa at Exeter Hall, where I remember enjoying immensely her faultless rendering of " With verdure clad ".

She was, moreover, a beautiful interpreter of Lieder. There, again, her dreamy, poetic manner and lyrical fervour cheated one into the belief that she was actuated by deep feeling. I had an opportunity once of watching this at close quarters at the house of her intimate friend Madame Balfe, the widow of the composer. She had " dropped in " for afternoon tea, and only a few people were there. Being in the mood to sing, she asked me to accompany her (*minus* music) in Schubert's " Ständchen " (or " Serenade "). She sang it beautifully in the original German, and with a tenderness that brought the tears to some of her listeners' eyes. To my ear, somehow, it sounded like the mechanical sentiment of a lovely *vox humana* stop without its objectionable *tremolo* ; yet no doubt she was putting into it all that she was *capable* of feeling.

She was a clever actress, and could meet the dramatic exigencies of the heaviest rôles, even if not wholly convincing in the depth of her sincerity. She had delightful variety and there were many salient episodes which she never played twice alike ; such, for example, as the prison scenes in *Faust* and *Mefistofele*, and that where Mignon decks herself in Filina's finery. She stamped her characters with an individuality of her own that drew admiration from critics like Clément and Pougin in Paris, Hanslick in Vienna, and those of the other European capitals where she was regularly fêted.

Her Cherubino pleased the Parisians, whilst London preferred Pauline Lucca's. Santley, with his customary candour, said what he thought about it in his *Reminiscences* : " It was pleasant to hear the music in the proper keys, but the impersonation was not a success. She (Nilsson) wore a nondescript dress which spoiled her figure ; instead of a sprightly page, she looked exactly what she was, a woman dressed in male attire, and very unhappy without the petticoats ". I never saw her, either, as the Countess in *Figaro*.[1] But her mastery of the classical style was made sufficiently manifest in *Don Giovanni* by her glorious " Mi tradì " and, I may add, by her magnificent rendering of Beethoven's " Ah, perfido ! " at the Philharmonic Concert of July 11th, 1870, in honour of the centenary of the composer's birth.

During the latter eventful year Nilsson paid her

[1] This part, like her Mignon, Nilsson sang for the first time in England at Drury Lane, in the same season (1870) that she first appeared here as Alice.

first visit to America, and toured there in concerts and opera under Maurice Strakosch. She quickly became a favourite and made herself a great name by, among other things, her embodiment of Marguerite.[1] For many successive years she continued to make profitable tours in the States, and concerning her co-operation in Henry E. Abbey's opening season at the Metropolitan Opera House, in 1883, Krehbiel wrote: " Mme Nilsson had been thirteen years before the American public, and though in this period her art had grown in dignity and nobility, her voice had lost the fresh bloom of its youth, and her figure had begun to take on matronly contours. Still, she was a great favourite, and hers was an extraordinary triumph, the outburst of popular approbation coming, as was to have been expected, in the garden scene of the opera (*Faust*) ".

5

She was twice married : first, in 1872, to a Frenchman, M. Auguste Rouzeaud (the wedding taking place on July 27th at Westminster Abbey), who died in February 1882 ; then in March 1887, to Count Casa de Miranda ; and this second union was the signal for her retirement from professional life. She gave two farewell concerts in London at the Albert Hall in the

[1] Writing on this subject in his *Chapters of Opera*, the late H. E. Krehbiel said :
" Twenty-five years ago there was no opera in the current repertory comparable in popularity with *Faust*. . . . To that popularity Mme Nilsson contributed a factor of tremendous puissance. No singer who is still a living memory was so intimately associated in the local mind with Gounod's masterpiece as she . . . who set the standard by which, for a long time, all subsequent representatives of the character were judged ".

summer of 1888, one under the direction of Mr
Kuhe on May 31st, when she was assisted by, among
others, Trebelli, Sims Reeves, and Sir George (then
Mr) Henschel; the second on June 20, at which the
supporting vocal artists included Antoinette Sterling,
Sims Reeves, Edward Lloyd, Santley, and Foli.
Except when she came out of her retirement to sing
at the Sims Reeves farewell in 1891, she never again
appeared in public in this country.

Early in the spring of 1887 I accompanied Sir
Augustus Harris to Madrid, where he went to choose
some artists for his tentative season of Italian opera at
Drury Lane.   His conductor, Luigi Mancinelli, was
presiding at the Royal Opera-house, and among others
a youthful baritone named Battistini was one of the
singers engaged.   We were invited to luncheon by the
British Ambassador, Sir Clare Ford, and I found to my
delight that the Countess de Miranda was one of the
guests.   She was on the Ambassador's right, and
graciously asked that I might sit next to her.   She had
then been married only a few weeks and declared
that she had looked forward with real pleasure to
relinquishing her career for good.   She added:

" I have not been at it so long as some singers, I
know; but I have worked hard ever since I was a
child, and 23 years of opera ought to be quite enough
for anyone.   So I have sold my house in Kensington
and settled down here in Madrid ".

" Do you like the life in Spain? " I asked.

" Yes, all but the bull-fights, which are horrible.   I
have promised my husband to go to one to-morrow;
but fortunately it is a charity affair, got up by the
Duchess d'Alva, and the whole performance is carried
out by amateurs.   They say they won't kill any horses,

and perhaps they may not even succeed in killing any bulls ! *Mais ça me dégoûte, tout de même."*

Later the Ambassador procured Sir Augustus a couple of tickets for this bull-fight, and we duly went. Of course it was not the kind of *correo* to attract the usual crowd of *aficionados ;* consequently the huge Plaza de Toros was not half filled. Having found the Count and Countess, we remained with them for the " show ". But the resolute lady kept her beautiful old fan well in front of her eyes, and never once did she glance at the bull-ring.

Early in the nineties I came across our " Swedish Nightingale " at Monte Carlo—a victim by then to the gambler's lure as well as to a pronounced *embonpoint.* But the deep-set blue eyes and the captivating smile still recalled the Christine Nilsson of old—the Alice in *Robert le Diable* of my boyhood's days. That meeting at Monte Carlo was the last time I saw her. She died in 1921 at the ripe age of 78, thus outliving her illustrious rival, Adelina Patti, by three years.

CHAPTER VI

ILMA DI MURSKA

THE BRILLIANT BUT ECCENTRIC

I

A PHENOMENAL singer and a pure eccentric, Ilma di Murska was by no means the least remarkable among the cantatrices who came " out of the wilds " in the mid-sixties. For a dozen years or more she stood her ground with the greatest *coloratura* artists of a unique epoch ; never posing as a rival of Adelina Patti or Pauline Lucca, who had both preceded her to London, nor of Christine Nilsson, who was to follow her after a couple of seasons ; yet boasting quite a multitude of admirers who knew a vocal genius when they heard one.

To-day Ilma di Murska would have provided pages of what journalists call " useful copy ". I often wonder what she would have thought of snapshots, gossip-pars, and publicity bureaux. It used to be surmised that she remained callous alike to the pæans of praise and the shafts of ridicule that were constantly being directed, now at the artist, now at the woman. On the other hand, Sir Charles Santley, who sang with her a good deal, relates in his book that there was one point on which she was extremely sensitive, namely, the subject of age.

One evening during a performance of *The Magic Flute* he found her sobbing violently in the wings, because someone in the company had slandered her by stating that she was 45. (As a matter of fact she was at that moment little more than 30.) He adds, " She had barely time to dry her eyes when she had to go on the stage; her grief, however, did not seem to affect her powers, for, to my astonishment, she sang as well as ever. No other singer whom I have heard, except Jenny Lind, sang the slow movement of ' Non paventar' (the Queen of Night's first air) as well as Di Murska ".[1]

But, after all, the *chronique scandaleuse des coulisses* in the sixties was purveyed almost exclusively by word of mouth. Not until years later did the modern musical Pepys begin to ornament his printed recollections with personal anecdotes of the gossipy or spicy order; and by that time the provocative Ilma was well out of reach. Each memoir-writer in turn, however, refers in detail to certain domestic habits and peculiarities that distinguished her from the current type of prima donna. None of them, for instance, mentions her without recalling the famous " large dog of uncertain breed " that used to accompany her on her walks and even to her rehearsals at the theatre. Her manager, Mapleson, assured us that she " travelled with an entire menagerie. Her immense Newfoundland, Pluto, dined with her every day. A cover was laid for him as for her, and he had learned to eat a fowl from a plate without dropping any of the meat or bones on the floor or even on the tablecloth. Pluto was a good-natured dog, or he would have made short work of the monkey, the two parrots, and the Angora

[1] *Student and Singer*, by Charles Santley.

cat who were his constant associates. The intelligent animal hated travelling in the dog-truck and he would resort to any sort of device in order to join his mistress in her first-class carriage, where he would, in spite of his immense bulk, squeeze himself beneath the seat ".

Luigi Arditi, again, had his word about Ilma di Murska: "Although her dramatic talent sometimes bordered on the extravagant, she was a remarkable actress as well as a brilliant singer. I remember, too, that she was rather eccentric and fond of ostentation, and that her dresses were invariably showy. One day she called upon us and we were really amazed at her appearance. To begin with she was accompanied by a huge black Swiss mountain dog (her constant companion), and gave one the impression of being clad in a dress similar to the Hungarian hussar costume. She wore her blonde hair reaching to her waist, while on her head was an imitation of the hussar busby, slightly on one side ".

2

Such were the grown-up characteristics of this strange Croatian girl concerning whose early history nothing has transpired beyond the fact (officially confirmed) that she was born at Agram in 1835. When she went to Vienna at the age of twenty-five, to study singing at the Conservatoire with Mme Mathilde Marchesi, she was already married to a Major-Auditor Eder and was the mother of two children. She had, however, been separated from her husband, and was therefore free to accompany her teacher when, in September, 1861, Mme Marchesi went to take up her residence in Paris. By then she must have been fairly advanced in her studies, for, only six months elapsed before she made her début.

According to her teacher, "Ilma di Murska had not only a sweet, flexible and high soprano voice (with a compass of nearly three octaves), but was also very musical and a quick learner. . . . She made an extraordinarily successful début as Martha at the Pergola Theatre, Florence, in April, 1862. Ilma soon became one of the most popular and celebrated of singers; but unfortunately she had a number of eccentricities—some of them harmless, while others seriously affected her health and her career". And then the inevitable reference to Pluto !

The successful start at Florence was followed by a tour in Southern Italy and Spain (Barcelona), after which the new singer's progress was interrupted by a serious illness, brought on by overwork. In 1863 she was once more winning triumphs at Budapest, Berlin, and Hamburg. At the Hofoper at Vienna she obtained a lengthy engagement and achieved celebrity as an interpreter of most of the leading *bravura* rôles. It was during this important period of her career that she gained, by daily association with artists of the first rank and constant changes of opera, the experience and all-round capacity which made her so valuable a recruit by the time she joined the Mapleson troupe at Her Majesty's Theatre in 1865.

She made her first appearance here on May 11th in *Lucia di Lammermoor* and, "at once took high rank from her phenomenal vocal qualities". Even more striking was the impression subsequently created by the unsurpassable ease and accuracy of her execution as the Queen of Night in a famous revival of Mozart's *Flauto Magico*. The cast further included Tietjens as

Pamina, Sinico as Papagena, Santley as Papageno, Bettini as Tamino, Trebelli as a Dama d'Onore, Rokitanski as Sarastro, and Foli, the famous Irish basso (making his début that season), as the Second Priest.

To hear Ilma di Murska sing the *Magic Flute* airs was regarded as among the notable events not to be missed in the operatic world. My own chance of enjoying this experience came during the George Wood season at Drury Lane Theatre in 1870, after I had seen her as Isabella in *Roberto il Diavolo* (see page 67). Two points I remember particularly—her regal appearance and unattractive looks as the Sicilian princess, and her magnificent rendering of the then-hackneyed aria, " Roberto, tu che adoro ! " She was, truly, an adept of the Meyerbeer school, as London was to prove later on when she appeared as the Queen in *Les Huguenots,* as Inez in *L'Africaine,* and, best of all, in *Dinorah*. The character and music of the half-demented Breton peasant-girl were exactly suited to her personality.

In short, as one of her critics has said, she was " unrivalled in certain romantic and fantastic characters ".[1] Her Dinorah was only one striking example of this faculty. Her mad scenes in *Lucia, Hamlet,* and *Linda di Chamouni* were other instances in point; and, not least of all, her fine Senta in Wagner's *Flying Dutchman,* when given for the first time in England at Drury Lane in 1870, with Santley in the part of Vanderdecken.

In the rôle of the Queen of Night I heard her more than once. In that trying part no one—not even

---

[1] Sutherland Edwards, *The Prima Donna.*

Marcella Sembrich—ever in my experience approached Ilma di Murska. The exceptionally lofty range of her voice enabled her to cope effortlessly with the octave leading to the F in *alt*. She simply revelled in it; making every note as clear, strong, and dramatic, as pure and ringing in tone, as the two octaves below that; thus forming a wholly perfect 3-octave scale. Her extraordinary voice and marvellous technique combined, together with a superb declamatory method, to impart to the " Non paventar " (as Santley declared) and also to the second aria, " Gli angui d'inferno ", the veritable tragic force and significance which Mozart intended these airs—too frequently treated as mere vocal exercises—to convey. In my opinion di Murska constituted in the purely vocal sense a reincarnation of Mozart's sister-in-law, Mme Hofer (the lady with the " voluble throat "), for whom this music was written.

3

In Italian Opera in the seventies an Italian title was a *sine quâ non*. *Der Fliegende Hollander* at Drury Lane was dubbed *L'Olandese Dannato ;* and at Covent Garden, seven years later, *Il Vascello Fantasma*. But the earlier production excited a merely lukewarm interest. The public treated the event with as much indifference as the three other important novelties—*Mignon* with Christine Nilsson, Mozart's *L'Oca del Cairo*, and Weber's *Abu Hassan*—which enriched the same financially disastrous season. Things had improved somewhat by the autumn of 1876, when Carl Rosa brought out the *Flying Dutchman* in English at the Lyceum with tremendous success. By then, however, we had heard *Lohengrin* and *Tannhäuser* in Italian and had begun to appreciate the Bayreuth master at something nearer his true worth.

Santley's own story of the Drury Lane production demands quotation here for the intimate picture it gives of Ilma di Murska's share in it. He says:

"*The Flying Dutchman* was not brought out until ten days before the close of the season. I thought it was going to be shelved, and I was anxious to play Vanderdecken, as I felt sure it was a part which would suit me well. I found Ilma di Murska, who was to be the Senta, was partly the cause of the delay, so I asked her plainly where her objection lay, and after a little beating about the bush she said— because it was all Flying Dutchman, while Senta was nobody. I told her she was wrong, that Senta was of quite as much importance as the Dutchman, for without Senta he certainly would be nobody. She afterwards altered her mind when she came to look into the part, and we worked together very earnestly at all the stage business. The audience from their applause showed they enjoyed the performance. Wagner, however, failed to attract the public. We only played it two or three nights, and to very poor houses. . . .

"Ilma di Murska was better suited with the part of Senta than with any part I saw her play. She looked it to per-fection; the weird, earnest, yet dreamy expression on her face denoted a spirit ready to make the sacrifice that was to be demanded of her—to give her life to save the soul of the unhappy man whose curse it was to wander until he should find a being capable of such a sacrifice. She acknowledged the mistake she had at first made, and played with an energy and spirit I had never before seen her display".

Sutherland Edwards made a special reference in his book to di Murska's "exceptional memory", observ-ing that "she remembered her parts, not like many untaught singers, from the sound of the tones, but from the aspect of the notes ". This confirms the opinion expressed by Mme Marchesi with regard to her musicianship and her ability to learn quickly. But concerning her histrionic gifts and her originality, the English critic added : " Mlle di Murska never ceases to hold the attention of her audience. She is full of life, and every one of her gestures, and even glances, is significant. Sometimes, no doubt, she exaggerates, now in one direction, now in another; but she is never cold and never leaves the public unmoved. . . . The originality which distinguished Ilma di Murska on the stage was occasionally shown by her in private life. She turned up in the most unexpected places, and when she first visited London, she gave a ball, which, beginning after the same night's performance, was (according to the invitations) to be carried on until an advanced hour next morning, and then followed by a picnic in Kew Gardens. An early visitor to Kew Gardens on the morning in question is prepared to certify that at the appointed hour no signs of the promised picnic were to be seen ".

4

Ilma di Murska's career after 1871 ceased to have any direct interest for London opera-goers. Her place at Her Majesty's was taken by Marie Marimon, while by the following year another notable high soprano, Emma Albani, was to make a brilliant début at Covent Garden. Seeking fresh laurels in America and the Antipodes, di Murska remained absent from this country for eight years and then returned only for a brief stay. Meanwhile she had married at Sydney in 1875 her second husband, Alfred Anderson, and, after

his death in the following year, her third, J. T. Hill, at
Otago, New Zealand. Unfortunately, in the course
of these marital experiences she lost the greater part
of her extensive earnings and came back to Europe a
comparatively poor woman. A return to the stage at
this juncture was out of the question. In 1880 she
accepted a professorship of singing at the National
Conservatory of Music in New York, but did not
retain it for long. Teaching, indeed, was never her
métier. Soon after came a peculiarly tragic ending.

Disappointed with life, "broken in body and
spirit", thwarted in her dearest ambitions, she left
America and went to live at Munich with her married
daughter, Frau von Czedic.[1] There her health
gradually failed, and on January 14, 1889, she died;
while her devoted daughter, inconsolable at her loss,
was so maddened by grief that she took poison and
expired a few hours later. Mother and daughter were
buried in the same grave at Gotha. If she bequeathed
nothing else, Ilma di Murska left behind her a great
name. At an epoch when song-goddesses were no
rarity, she won for herself a prominent niche in the
operatic Hall of Fame.

---

[1] One of the two children Ilma di Murska had taken to
Vienna in 1860, when she went to study with Marchesi. According-
ing to the latter, the daughter was also one of her pupils and
occupied a position in Munich "as a talented singer and
authoress ".

CHAPTER VII
THE ENCHANTING ZELIA TREBELLI

I

THE " beloved sister artist " of Theresa Tietjens—
Zelia Trebelli—was entitled to be so-called by virtue
of long association and closest ties of affection. But
as the " successor of Alboni " she ought never to have
been described. She possessed neither the deep range
of a genuine contralto nor the masculine tenor-like
tone that distinguished the voice of the renowned
Italian. Trebelli's compass was nearly as extraordinary
as Alboni's ; that is to say, it covered two-and-a-half
octaves, from the G flat below middle C to the D
flat in *alt*. Her timbre, however, was that of a typical
mezzo-soprano, with the stronger volume tending
towards the upper, not the lower register. As a matter
of fact, she produced her notes with such ease throughout the scale that she could and did sing music written
for almost any kind of voice ; and she was naturally
obliged to take the contralto parts both in opera and
oratorio. Hence the error.

Another point : Trebelli, who was a beautiful and
fascinating woman, impersonated upon the stage many
more male than female characters, and was probably
more completely at home in the former than in the
latter. Certainly no one else looked half so well as she
in parts like Cherubino (*Le Nozze di Figaro*), Maffio

Orsini (*Lucrezia Borgia*), Arsace (*Semiramide*), Urbano (*Les Huguenots*), Un Caprajo (*Dinorah*), Siebel (*Faust*), or Frédéric (*Mignon*). She had the art of striking the attitudes characteristic of a boy, and of moving about the stage and making gestures like one. On one occasion, " to oblige the management ", she actually sang (and acted with immense spirit) the tenor rôle of Tamino in *Il Flauto Magico*. More than once she displayed her unusual versatility by undertaking Almaviva in *Il Barbiere di Siviglia*. (It was not my good fortune to be present when she performed either of those *tours de force ;* but she possessed such a wonderful ear that I always realized her ability to pick up correctly any music that she had heard once or twice.) Like the renowned Malibran (a mezzo-contralto) she was well suited by the music of Rosina, and I heard her in that character at Her Majesty's. It was in fact a favourite rôle of Trebelli's.

Nevertheless it was not true, though frequently stated, that she made her début on the operatic stage as Rosina, with Mario in the part of Almaviva. That début took place at the Madrid Opera House in 1859, and the opera was *Il Trovatore*, the illustrious Mario being the Manrico. Verdi's early work, then barely six years old, had become the rage all over Europe; and the alluring charm of this new and youthful Azucena, associated as she was with such a Manrico, roused the Spaniards to an unwonted pitch of enthusiasm. The fact is worth recalling, not only out of consideration for historical accuracy, but because Azucena was the part which Trebelli was singing most frequently everywhere with Tietjens and was therefore the one in which she was best known to British audiences. The many other operas in which these

TREBELLI AS THE PAGE ("LES HUGUENOTS")

two artists appeared together need not for the moment
be enumerated. Enough that the public was in the
habit of associating the names of Tietjens and Trebelli
as one would those of Orestes and Pylades or Castor
and Pollux. The artistic union of the two singers
endured for fifteen years.

2

It was at Paris, in 1838, that Zélie or Zelia Trebelli
(she always signed herself " Zelia ") first saw the light.
Hers was a *nom de théâtre* derived from the family
name of Gillebert, spelt backwards and omitting the
G. At a very early age she gave signs of becoming
a musical prodigy and was trained as a pianist, but
without being allowed to play in public. Her possession of an exceptional voice was not discovered until
she was sixteen, and then only through an " accident ",
the story of which she has thus related :

" I was a good accompanist, and obtained an engagement
to act in that capacity in the studio of M. Pierre Wartel,[1]
the well-known teacher (who was later on to train Christine
Nilsson). One day a pupil failed to keep her appointment
and M. Wartel quitted the teaching-room for his study,
where he began writing letters. Left alone, I amused myself
by singing a couple of songs. The *maître*, supposing his
pupil to have at length arrived, presently returned. I
immediately ceased singing, but M. Wartel insisted on my
repeating a verse of the second song. He then seated himself at the piano and made me do some scales and sustained

[1] Fétis mentions in his *Biographie Universelle* that Wartel was
himself a pupil of the famous tenor, Nourrit, and that he sang at
the Opéra for about fifteen years (1831–46). He adds, " *Au nombre
des élèves qu'il a formés on remarque particulièrement la cantatrice
Mlle. Trebelli* ".

tones. He liked my voice well enough to predict for me a successful future in opera, and generously offered to teach me for nothing. My parents were not less delighted than I was, and we gratefully accepted. I studied under Wartel for five years ".

From the studio she went straight to the stage, making her début, as already noted, at Madrid in 1859. Her success attracted the attention of the impresario Merelli, who used at that time to tour the Continent with a strong Italian company, and was subsequently to present Adelina Patti in the principal cities of Holland, Germany, and Austria. He offered an engagement to the new mezzo-soprano, and, during 1860-6 she added strength and lustre to his troupe, among other things completely conquering the hearts of the difficult public of Berlin and Vienna. In March, 1862, she sang at one of the Gewandhaus Concerts at Leipzig, and roused her critical audience to such unwonted transports of delight that she was immediately engaged by Mapleson for London, where she promptly made her first appearance at Her Majesty's Theatre.

With her advent in this, the land of her adoption, the real career of Zelia Trebelli may be said to have begun. She was now twenty-four; a singularly handsome, graceful Frenchwoman, and full of charm. She had bright, eloquent, intelligent eyes and an unusually pretty mouth, with lips that could expand into the most captivating of smiles. She made her début (May 9th, 1862) as Maffio Orsini in *Lucrezia Borgia*, Tietjens, of course, being the Lucrezia, and instantly won all hearts by her fascinating embodiment of the dashing young noble. Four nights later she " drove the nail home " with her picturesque and dramatic assumption of Azucena, sharing honours not only then with Tietjens and Giuglini, but also later on with her countryman Naudin, the fine heroic tenor who was soon afterwards to create the rôle of Vasco da Gama in *L'Africaine*.

When I heard her for the first time (eight years later) as Arsace in *Semiramide*, her voice had, I was told, developed a greater roundness and opulence of tone than it possessed when she first came here. It did not, however, strike me as being so remarkable for its power as for its purity and richness. In Rossini's florid music one noted more especially the matchless evenness of her scale. Above all, there was a curious lovable quality such as a great 'cellist will sometimes caress from his instrument, together with a ring of tenderness and pathos which at moments would bring a " lump " to the throat. To the individual timbre was allied a rare elegance of phrasing, an extraordinary breadth and nobility of expression, the whole suggesting that wonderful combination—a French training based upon the finest attributes of the old Italian School.

Trebelli had from the outset profited substantially by her association with the gifted singers then engaged at Her Majesty's—Tietjens, Nilsson, Ilma di Murska, Giuglini, Faure, Santley, and Agnesi, to mention only a few. In the performance of *Semiramide* Tietjens, Trebelli, and Agnesi made a matchless trio of Rossinian artists—one worth making a long journey to listen to. The rendering of the duet, " Giorno d'orrore ", with its *rococo* trills in thirds and sixths, dwells ineffaceably in the memory. The majestic Tietjens was rather taller than Trebelli; but, on the other hand, Arsace was much better-looking than his unsuspected mother, and made love to her with an intensity of passion that almost lent *vraisemblance* to the ancient story. At the date I am speaking of these two " inseparables " had sung together in some twenty operas ; and no matter what the school or who the composer, they were equally at home and perfect in all.

3

Quick to learn, quick to imitate and retain, it was not surprising that an immense difference in Trebelli's art should have been noticed after her first two or three seasons in London. Her technique was already polished, but constant work and experience had made of her a highly finished artist. The consummate ease that distinguished her method of producing her voice, the delicate refinement of her ornamentation, and her brilliant feats of *bravura* earned the unqualified eulogy of the most exacting critics. Truth to tell, she had been a favourite from the beginning, and on her first return in 1863, she began to perceive good reasons for making her permanent home in London. Not the least of these was the fact that she had fallen in love with one of Mr Mapleson's best Italian tenors, Signor Alessandro Bettini, and he with her. In course of the summer they were married.

Then 1863 was also the *Faust* year. Gounod, who was warmly attached to Trebelli, persuaded her to add the comparatively small part of Siebel to her growing gallery of male characters, and came over expressly for the first representation of his opera at Her Majesty's on June 11th. Her performance " was a happy combination of excellent singing and refined artistic acting ". Side by side with Tietjens, Giuglini, Gassier, and Santley, she reaped her full share in the honours of an historic occasion; lending, moreover, personal attraction and musical interest to a part that others have seldom succeeded in making aught but colourless and insipid.

Gounod was so delighted with Trebelli and with Santley that he offered to write an additional song for each of them. The outcome was Siebel's " When all was young " and Valentine's " Even bravest hearts may swell ". In the autumn Mapleson made a recital of *Faust* the feature of his provincial concert tour, and in this Trebelli's husband took the title-rôle. Thereafter she was always known as Mme Trebelli-Bettini, even when, a few years later, the pair found each other to be suffering from incompatibility of temper and agreed to separate.

Mapleson has related how Bettini once helped him out in a stage performance of *Faust* for which he had engaged Sims Reeves. Of course the eminent English tenor disappointed; that was his unfortunate habit. Amid the complications that ensued, the regular members of the cast somehow got dreadfully upset—Trebelli so badly that she had to go home to bed. Bettini did not know the whole of the part of Faust (the opera in 1864 being still practically new) nor did the other available tenor, Volpini. Nevertheless Mapleson hoped that between them " they might manage to get through it ". But how to find another Siebel? He tells the story thus :

" It was now half-past eight, and the opera was on the point of commencing. Meanwhile I had followed Mdme. Trebelli to her apartments in Regent Street. The excitement had made her quite ill, and she was totally unable to appear in consequence. I appealed forcibly to her husband, begging him, if he would not sing Faust, to help me by taking the part of Siebel. He was a very good musician, and as at this time he never quitted his wife's side, I knew that he must be intimately acquainted with the music. I thereupon got him down to the theatre in time for the garden scene, had his moustache taken off and put him into his wife's clothes. Everything went off brilliantly "—

including, I suppose, the moustache !

4

Trebelli was a woman of delightful disposition. Amiable and kind to a fault, she was a loyal friend, an artist ever faithful to her manager, singularly free from the foibles and intrigues of the ordinary operatic artist. She never gave trouble, but was always willing to strengthen the ensemble by undertaking an insignificant rôle when required. In Mozart's *Magic Flute* it was her custom—Tietjens being the Pamina—to sing the part of the third Lady or Damigella della Regina. No character and no music came amiss to her, except when she essayed Carmen late in her career. Following closely upon Minnie Hauk's vivid embodiment when the opera was first done here in 1878, she proved too refined, too " ladylike ", for Bizet's capricious heroine. Even so, however, her superb singing of music that suited her well saved her from actual failure.

Her Zerlina in *Don Giovanni*, delightful for its piquant freshness and vivacity, was found worthy to shine beside the Donna Anna of Tietjens and the Donna Elvira of Nilsson. She would brighten the stage for ten minutes as the Goatherd in *Dinorah*, to sing " *Fanciulle che il core* " as no one but herself or Scalchi has ever sung it. Her Page in *Les Huguenots* was inimitable; her dashing delivery of "Nobil signor" something that has never been quite equalled. As Maddalena she infused her own peculiar charm into the last act of *Rigoletto* and imparted an unforgettable touch to her share in the famous quartet; there was a world of coquetry in her phrasing of the line, "*Il vostro giuoco so apprezzar*". ("I know how to value your jest").

To her Maffio Orsini reference may again be made. It was perhaps the most characteristic of her assumptions; and, so long as Tietjens lived to sing Lucrezia Borgia, so long did Trebelli continue to entrance us with Orsini's youthful exuberance and defiant high spirits. She never failed to carry away her audience with the popular *brindisi* or to electrify them with the boldness of her attack and rhythm in the ensemble, "Maffio Orsini, signori, son io!" Worth recalling, too, were her splendid Fatima in the revival of Weber's *Oberon* in the early seventies, with Tietjens magnificent as Rezia; her weird Ulrica in the *Ballo in Maschera*; her humorous Nancy in *Martha*; her Neris in Cherubini's *Medea* (also revived for Tietjens); her Pierotto in *Linda di Chamouni*; and her tragic Leonora in *La Favorita*. Last but not least, one may mention her rare modesty in taking a small part like Frasquita for the first performance of *Carmen*.

As a concert vocalist, Trebelli's career in this country owed its unbroken success almost as much to her winning personality as to her extraordinary versatility, to her complete mastery of oratorio and its cognate branches. I remember her exquisite rendering of the air for David, "O Lord, whose mercies" (from *Saul*), at the Handel Festival of 1874. Not long after she was enchanting us with the "Habañera" from

Carmen, which she introduced to an English audience two years before the opera was brought out at Her Majesty's.

Her first appearance at one of the great provincial Festivals was at Norwich in 1863. Not having studied oratorio as yet, she only took part in the "miscellaneous" programmes, making a half-unperceived début in the quintet from *Un Ballo in Maschera*. Next season she was the vocalist at a Philharmonic Concert[1] and afforded with her operatic arias an apt illustration of the "miscellaneous" Philharmonic vocal taste of those days. Among other things, she achieved somewhat of a *tour de force* (for a reputed contralto) by singing the "Jewel Song" from *Faust!*—quite an exciting novelty at that epoch, to be sure!

5

It was in 1885 that Mme Trebelli first invited me to visit her at her house in Morpeth Terrace, opposite the Westminster Cathedral. In private life she was a merry, fascinating hostess, remarkable for her pungent, witty conversation and *spirituel* talk about her art. Her avoidance of self-assertion or conceit was not less noticeable at home than in the opera house. She had a villa at Étretat, but only spent her holidays there. When I asked her once why she did not sing more on the Continent she exclaimed, "I only love my dear English public! That is why I go abroad so rarely

---

[1] In his *History of the Philharmonic Society of London*, Myles Birket Foster described Trebelli as "one of the most charming, sympathetic and popular contralto operatic singers, and, above all, an excellent musician, who, between this year (1864) and 1876, sang at ten of the concerts".

to sing, though I am often asked to.   If I spend the summer at Étretat I am always glad to get back to London and my work ".   She was not a very happy woman just then, though her vivacious manner and high spirits would scarcely have allowed one to guess it.

She always loved a bit of fun.   I recollect one Sunday evening, shortly after her daughter Antoinette's return from Brussels (where she had been studying to be a singer[1]), someone suggested a little music.   " So long as it's jolly ", said Trebelli, " we'll have as much as you like.   Let me begin with my new song ! "   And with that she dashed off into the refrain of Denza's Neapolitan ditty, " Funiculi, funicula ".   Antoinette and the rest of us joined in *fortissimo*, making a din that must have aroused the neighbourhood.   Half a dozen times I thought we had ended ; but no, Trebelli would always start off afresh, until at last she had to stop from sheer exhaustion through singing and laughing so long.

In pursuit of her art she never knew the meaning of fatigue.   In 1878 she went to New York for the first time as a member of Mapleson's troupe, and again in 1883 to sing under Henry Abbey during the opening season at the Metropolitan Opera House.   During both visits she was working night after night both on the stage and at concerts.   Back in London, she stuck loyally to her old manager (after the death of Tietjens), together with Nilsson, Campanini, Del Puente, and

[1] Antoinette Trebelli, also known as Antoinette Dolores, made her début in 1886, and sang for several years at London concerts and in South Africa, where she became a great favourite. She had a flexible, musical soprano voice and used it with notable skill and agility.

the rest; and among other parts she sang the dual rôles of Marta and Pantalis in *Mefistofele* when Boito's masterpiece was produced at Her Majesty's in 1880. Six years later she was assisting in what proved to be Mapleson's final season at that house; nor shall I readily forget the enthusiastic reception that she had on the second night in her old part of Siebel. Her voice sounded very nearly as fresh and strong as ever, and her style had all the winning grace of old.

To wind up, we find her in May 1888, appearing two or three times at Covent Garden under the management of Augustus Harris; and appropriately enough, it was in her old part of Maffio Orsini that she made what proved to be all but her farewell. For *Lucrezia* was given on the opening night—alas, without Tietjens !—Fursch-Madi being in the title-rôle. A few nights later, the "evergreen artist and favourite", as one critic described her, sang Siebel in *Faust* as she alone could. And that was the end. We were never to hear her in opera again.

She had a paralytic seizure in 1889 which, although it incapacitated her from further public work, was not immediately followed by a fatal termination. After a long rest she was able to take up the (to her) not uncongenial labour of teaching, for her mental faculties remained strong. I saw her more than once during that period and found she was taking all her accustomed interest in the musical affairs of the day. She even ventured, on May 30th, 1892, to appear before an audience once more at the annual concert given at St. George's Hall by her staunch friend, Mme Puzzi, a celebrated figure of that period. In the following June she died, on the night of the 17th, whilst at her villa at Étretat.

Her health had improved; but an unusually violent thunderstorm came on at about midnight and prevented her from sleeping. Towards 3 a.m., whilst laughing and chatting with a favourite pupil, she had an attack of heart-failure and expired almost immediately. The funeral took place at Poissy, near Paris, in the presence of only a few near relatives and friends. Paris scarcely knew of her death, and there was no chance for a demonstration of personal affection such as had been witnessed fifteen years before at Kensal Green at the funeral of her faithful comrade. Yet it may be asserted without exaggeration that Zelia Trebelli, an artist almost as supreme in her line as Theresa Tietjens, had stood little lower in the esteem and regard of the British people.

CHAPTER VIII

EMMA ALBANI

CANADA'S FAMOUS SONGSTRESS

I

LONG and honourable was the career of this gifted woman and fine artist. Yet, sad to relate, the smiles of Fortune, which she enjoyed at one time in such generous measure, refused to come her way during the evening of her life. When she died in London on April 3, 1930, she was in her 80th year; and a span of exactly fifty-eight years stretched back to the spring of 1872 when she had made her début at Covent Garden.[1] So consistent a hard worker and popular a favourite unquestionably deserved ample reward for all her earnest striving. But the world knew well enough that the responsibility for that had not been hers.

It is not easy for the present generation to realize how distinguished a place Mme Albani filled in the estimation of the musical world in the closing decades of the last century. During the early seventies she was, so to speak, only one amongst many; for as has been

[1] Dame Emma Albani was born at Chambly, near Montreal, on November 1st, 1850, not 1852, as incorrectly stated in her book of reminiscences, *Forty Years of Song* (published in 1911). When she first appeared in London her age was accurately given as 22.

ALBANI AS SITA ("ROI DE LAHORE")

already observed, those were days when it was no facile business for the newcomer to fight her way to the front and hold her place there. Although, fortunately for her, Albani pleased her public from the first, there were stars like Patti, Tietjens, Nilsson, Lucca, Miolan-Carvalho, Marimon, Etelka Gerster, Bianca Bianchi, and Zaré Thalberg shining at their brightest, so that upward progress meant an incessant struggle. It was only after she had proved capable of excelling in the Wagnerian and later forms of modern opera—*i.e.*, in a new line of romantic characters which, more or less, differentiated her from her rivals—that she began to establish herself firmly and solidly in the favour of Mr Gye's patrons.

The ability to accomplish this she owed largely to her skill as a musician. The elder Lamperti had made an excellent singer of her, utilizing to the best advantage vocal resources by no means on a level with those of some of the superlative artists named above. But the capacity for accurate sight-reading of the most difficult scores, for playing the pianoforte well, for quickly committing new rôles to memory, for the sympathetic interpretation of the music of any school—all this she owed entirely to the rigorous technical training which her French-Canadian father, Joseph Lajeunesse, had imposed upon her in her childhood.

Her conspicuous talent as an actress might be accounted for in the same way; that is to say, not merely by natural inclination, but by the histrionic qualities which she acquired through imitating an elderly aunt who had a *flair* for telling lively stories with realistic action. And the power of imitation is one of the most helpful gifts bestowed upon mankind for the study of any art.

Growing up in a musical atmosphere and accustomed to displaying her precocious talent before local audiences, this Canadian girl was well prepared for the period of more serious study in Europe which she undertook by the advice of Prince Poniatowski, a well-known amateur composer. After six months in Paris under Duprez, the famous tenor, she went to Milan and worked under Lamperti, whose admirable method she thoroughly mastered. Then in 1870, on her twentieth birthday, she madea successful début at Messina, in Sicily, in *La Sonnambula*. She had adopted the *nom de théâtre* of Albani, not, as has often been stated, because of some connection with the town of Albany (New York State), but at the suggestion of her elocution teacher, who recommended it as being " the name of a distinguished Italian family, whose descendants were mostly dead ".

Her season at Messina ended, she followed it up with another public essay at Florence (where she met Jenny Lind) and a winter at Malta. The experience earned during these engagements was confined to *soprano leggiero* parts such as Amina, Elvira (*Puritani*), Lucia, Linda, Rosina, Isabella (*Roberto*), and Inez (*L'Africaine*). They were consequently regarded as her true *métier* when she first visited London in the summer of 1871 to seek an engagement at one of the opera-houses. It was then too late to make room for her at Covent Garden, but Mr Gye (her future father-in-law), having heard her sing, promised to include her in his company the following year. He kept his word. She made her début there on April 2, 1872, as Amina in *La Sonnambula,* and obtained a most cordial reception.

2

The story of Emma Albani's early seasons in England constitute an eloquent tribute not only to her artistic powers, but to the undaunted energy of her disposition and her resolute determination to succeed. That trait dated from her childhood in Canada, when her father—harpist, violinist and organist—her severe but kindly mentor on the borders of Lake Champlain —seems to have imbued her with the notion that she must one day stand second to none among the stars of the vocal firmament. Seeing how great were the obstacles, it was amazing how she came so nearly to accomplishing her design. Only a woman possessing unbounded ambition, allied to geniune talent and capacity for hard work, could have overcome the discouragements incidental to the long struggle against brilliant rivals. Ultimately perseverance and all-round ability enabled her to carry the position.

When, in 1878, she became the wife of Ernest Gye, her impresario's eldest son and "right hand man", she had become, if not actually *nulli secunda*, at any rate second to only one of the Covent Garden *prime donne assolute*, and that one Adelina Patti. She was sensible and diplomatic enough to draw the line at rivalry there, if nowhere else. By that time, too, she had found her true vocation as a lyric artist and ascertained that she could afford to leave to others the lighter rôles of the repertory. By degrees Amina and Lucia, Martha and Linda, Elvira and Gilda dropped out, while Elsa, Elisabeth and Senta, with Violetta, Marguerite, Countess Almaviva, and Desdemona, became the customary selection. But, before dwelling on these last, let me go back to some earlier impressions.

I heard Albani for the first time in 1874, her third season here, the opera being *Lucia di Lammermoor*. She was then 24; not precisely beautiful, either in face or figure, but endowed with a winning, intelligent expression, graceful in her gestures, and obviously possessing a strong sense of the theatre. Her voice, a soprano of considerable range, with fine notes in the head register, was then clear and resonant if somewhat thin in timbre; perhaps more remarkable for its flexibility and a remarkable *sostenuto* (due to perfect breath-control) than for that peculiar sweetness and charm which haunts the ear. Neither then nor subsequently was there much power in the chest and lower medium notes; indeed, it struck me that those registers had been somewhat sacrificed for the sake of adding resonance to the more acute section of the voice.

There were also—especially in her singing of the old Italian operas—certain peculiarities in the mode of attack as well as a tendency to unduly prolong prominent high notes (*points-d'orgue*, the French call them); and those peculiarities were destined to develop as time went on into mannerisms. On the other hand, in a technical sense her execution was neatness itself. The scales were even; and everything sounded right except the trill, which she had an odd way of executing a semitone higher and then returning to the correct note at the end.

I do not remember Albani in either of her French rôles, Mignon and Ophélie; nor, assuredly, did she sing either at Covent Garden during more than one or two early seasons. But in her Wagner-Italian creations at that house she was wholly admirable. I heard her (from a lofty perch among the " gods ") in the first productions in England of *Lohengrin* (1875) and *Tannhäuser* (1876); likewise in *The Flying Dutchman*, then called *Il Vascello Fantasma*, with Maurel as the Vanderdecken. If the music of *Lohengrin* was to us a revelation, no less so was Albani's Elsa. Apart from the glamour of the opera's complete novelty, alike as to music, orchestral colouring, and stage pictures, one recalls the vivid impression of a dreamy, poetic maiden, presenting a combination of womanly weakness and charm, caught in the toils of a romantic tragedy quite unlike the violent dramas usually encountered in the stilted regions of conventional opera. And the experience was at that epoch as delightful as it was novel.

What with the Italian surroundings of the theatre; the use of an Italian text; the two Frenchmen, Nicolini and Maurel (Lohengrin and Telramund); two Italians, d'Angeri and Bagagiolo (Ortrud and the King); and an Italian conductor in Vianesi, it seemed as though Emma Albani embodied as the heroine the only purely Teutonic realization of the Wagnerian ideal. Nor was this mere fancy; for the Canadian soprano had gone to Munich for a fortnight before the production, and carefully studied her rôle with the well-known conductor and " coach ", Franz Wüllner. He unquestionably succeeded in making her absorb the " atmosphere " of the character and the music. Her Elisabeth and Senta were almost equally admired, the former having also been studied with Herr Wüllner. All these rôles provided an object-lesson in the innocuousness of the new art of Wagnerian singing, which until then had been regarded as a means

for inevitably and incurably damaging the human
voice.[1]

3

When Theresa Tietjens died Albani took her place
as the leading oratorio soprano of this country. She
had been gradually but surely winning her way to that
position. Sir Julius Benedict, always closely associated with Mr Gye, had secured her an engagement
for the Norwich Festival of 1872, immediately following her initial season at Covent Garden. At that
gathering her work was restricted (as had been in the
case of Trebelli) to operatic items in the miscellaneous
programmes; but subsequently she was allowed a
better chance. I remember particularly her ringing
notes in the *Hymn of Praise* at the Festival of 1875,
when Tietjens also sang gloriously in the *Messiah*—for
the last time. Notable, too, were Albani's successes at
the Handel Festival of 1877 and the Gloucester
Festival in the same year, just before Tietjens was laid
to rest. After that the road was clear. Lemmens-
Sherrington had practically retired; while the expen-
sive super-stars, Patti and Nilsson, could only be
afforded for one or two concerts at the wealthier
Festivals.

Albani's oratorio style was at the outset singularly
pure and quite free from the mannerisms which marred
it in later years. Her resonant tones never failed to
penetrate to the farthest extremities of the largest
auditorium, whether the interior of one of our noble

---

[1] Another striking proof of the stupidity of this notion was
afforded by the fine singers who were heard at the Wagner
Festival at the Albert Hall in 1877.

cathedrals, the centre transept of the Crystal Palace, or the vast amphitheatre of the Albert Hall. The high note might be held a shade too long, but it was always dead in tune; nor was it heralded (in the concert room) by that invariable stage habit of raising the right arm whenever a slow *portamento* landed the voice somewhere " in the heights ".

Composers of new works eagerly sought her co-operation because she was a musician upon whom they could rely. Gounod rejoiced to have her for his *Redemption* and *Mors et Vita* at Birmingham; Dvorák for his *Stabat Mater* and *Spectre's Bride;* Sullivan for his *Martyr of Antioch* and *Golden Legend* at Leeds; Cowen for his *St. Ursula* at Norwich. She studied these new works with punctilious care, and realized the composers' intentions down to the finest point.

Her companions at most of the Festivals or the big oratorio performances were Madame Patey, Edward Lloyd, and Santley; and this distinguished group was generally known in the middle eighties as the " representative English quartet ". Elsewhere her associates would be Antoinette Sterling, Joseph Maas, Foli, or Frederic King; but, no matter which or where, the ensemble would have been difficult to match. One always felt in the case of Albani that the current of dramatic feeling was portrayed with the utmost sincerity; that her heartfelt earnestness was the outcome of genuine conviction. Her expression in the interpretation of religious music was never exaggerated, and often extremely touching.

Like Patti, she had the gift of pronouncing foreign languages as correctly as her own; she could sing equally well in English, French, Italian, or German. When she went to Berlin in 1887 to appear at the Royal

Opera she greatly surprised her audiences and the
critics by employing the German text both in *Lohengrin*
and *The Flying Dutchman*.   Shortly after that she sang
Elsie in Sullivan's *Golden Legend* when it was given for
the second time in Berlin under the composer's
direction.   The work had come very near to absolute
failure on the first occasion, owing chiefly to the
deficiencies of the local soprano.   Sir Arthur Sullivan
wrote telling me how Albani had hurried from
Antwerp at his urgent request and saved the situation
by a magnificent rendering of the part she had created
at the Leeds Festival in the previous year.   " It made ",
he said, " all the difference in the world.   She positively
sang her heart out, and, instead of showing the
utmost apathy, the Berliners received the work from
first to last with enthusiasm ".

I have somehow always associated Albani more
closely with her two heroines of the Scheldt and the
Rhine—Elsa and Elsie—than with any other characters
in her répertoire.   She was, however, charming in two
operatic parts that never became popular, both of
which she created here with the famous French baritone Lassalle (one on his début at Covent Garden in
1879), viz., Sita in *Il Re di Lahore*, by Massenet ; the
other, in 1881, Tamara in *Il Demonio*, by Anton
Rubinstein.   But neither work scored a success.

It was a little before then that she first appeared at
Covent Garden as the Countess in *Le Nozze di Figaro*,
and I remember in connection with that a little incident.   The rôle of Susanna was allotted to an accomplished young soprano, Bianca Bianchi, who was
afterwards a celebrity on the Continent, but had not
yet become a favourite in London.   In the duet,
" Sull'aria ", where the voices unite in a cadence

towards the end, Susanna sings up to the high B flat whilst the Countess sings a third lower, so that for the moment, as Mozart has willed it, the voice of the mistress is outshone by that of the maid. But that would not do for Albani, who, being then the mistress in every sense, politely requested her youthful *comprimaria* to take the G whilst she appropriated the top note.

For the stories of her manifold associations with Royalty in this country and with crowned heads everywhere else the reader may be referred to Dame Albani's book. She was *persona gratissima* at our own Court and an especial favourite with Queen Victoria. Both in the United States and in Canada, the land of her birth, her singing always evoked the heartiest enthusiasm; nor was there a town in the British Isles where she was not received with open arms. Her first tour through India, South Africa, and Australasia in 1898 was marked by a long series of ovations. The second, nine years later, was also highly successful, while in 1903 she paid her last visit to Canada. In 1911 she bade farewell to public life at an Albert Hall concert, and after that devoted herself for some years to the work of teaching. In 1925 King George bestowed upon her the distinction of a Dame of the British Empire.

Her parting words of advice, reproduced in facsimile in her autobiography, were so true and full of sense that I venture in conclusion to quote some of them here :

" I consider it necessary to obtain early complete mastery of music, so important in these days, a perfect diction in several languages, and a continual study of the ' Art of Singing ' as the old masters taught it, so that the natural beauty of the Instrument (voice) may be increased, greater power gained and complete control of the voice obtained. Need I add great perseverance in study and judicious hard work. However well artists may do, and no matter how much success they may have, they should always bear in mind that it is possible to do better, and should never relax their efforts to attain an ever-higher standard ".

CHAPTER IX

LILLIAN NORDICA

THE AMERICAN SOPRANO

I

FOREMOST among American operatic sopranos stands the name of the accomplished Lillian Nordica. She merits remembrance not only for her achievements as a lyric artist, but for her inestimable work as a pioneer. It was her indomitable energy and skill that made the path easier for those who came after her. Her predecessors, Annie Louise Cary and Clara Louise Kellogg, had done something, but not a great deal, to make the way smooth. The average fair American aspirant was, in the last quarter of the nineteenth century, still finding the hill to the Temple of Fame hard to climb.

It remained for a hardworking, resolute, ambitious New England girl to do the real " spade-work ". Sublimely ignorant, when she began, as to the gigantic nature of the task before her, she happily possessed plenty of talent and common sense (save where her heart was concerned), in addition to a clever business mind. Good looks also she had in plenty, a fine figure, and, for a girl, an astonishingly powerful high C. Everything, in short, was in her favour except experience (which she had to pay dearly for all her life) and sound musical training, when she started in the mid-seventies as a soprano soloist in Dr Putnam's church at Boston, Mass.

Her native town was Farmington, Maine, where she was born on May 12, 1859. When the family had moved to Boston she entered the new England Conservatory and studied singing under Mr John O'Neill. Then, when barely eighteen and long before she had completed her vocal equipment, her mother arranged for her to go on an extended concert tour with Theodore Thomas's Orchestra. Through that, however, and one or two appearances with the Handel and Haydn Society in Boston, she obtained confidence and the habit of singing before large audiences. Her fresh, bright, resonant voice and natural method of using it pleased everywhere.

Proud of her nationality, she sang under her family name of Lillian Norton. In 1878 she was engaged to tour as the vocalist with Patrick Gilmore's American Band, an organization akin to that which John P. Sousa was subsequently to form; and in that capacity, on a warm May day, she duly appeared in England at the Crystal Palace. Of this event one remembers as the outstanding feature a happy, smiling young girl, who tripped lightly up to the platform between the instrumental selections, and sang a couple of operatic arias and a ballad or two. From the London press, however, she received encouragement to undertake further study; consequently, instead of returning to the States, she went straight off to Milan, accompanied by her mother, to place herself under Sangiovanni, one of the most celebrated Italian teachers of the day. It was only then, in fact, that she definitely decided to adopt an operatic career; and, after twelve months'

Lillian Nordica 1891

NORDICA AS MARGUERITE

intensive training, she was pronounced ready for the plunge.

Under the stage name of Nordica, she made her début at Brescia as Violetta in *La Traviata* (April 30, 1879) and entered upon the romance that her chequered life was to unfold. Recognized as a lyric soprano of decided promise, she made the round of the leading Italian theatres with some success. In 1880 she obtained engagements in Germany and Russia, gradually gaining experience in parts like Lucia, Violetta, Gilda, Filina in *Mignon*, and Amelia in *Un Ballo in Maschera*. Another couple of years found her singing at the Paris Opéra, a friend and pupil of the two favourite composers Gounod and Ambroise Thomas. As a result she added Marguerite in *Faust* and Ophélie in *Hamlet* to her growing list of successes.

Then, unluckily, she fell in love with and married Frederick A. Gower, the scientist and aeronaut of " Gower-Bell " fame, and, in obedience to his wish, forthwith quitted her public career. A few months later her husband lost his life in an attempt to cross the English Channel in a balloon, and his body was never recovered.

2

The name of Lillian Nordica was for a time in danger of being forgotten. During the early days of her widowhood, she had given no sign of a desire to return to the operatic stage, when suddenly, in 1885, she reappeared in the States under the management of James Henry Mapleson. He had been carrying on a long season in New York, followed by an extended tour, which proved a financial failure. But Nordica remained with her new impresario throughout the venture and subsequently followed him to London. There he started a season of Italian opera at cheap prices at Covent Garden on March 12th, 1887.

There, also, among other parts, she sang Gilda to the Rigoletto of M. Lhérie—whose name is worth recalling because he was the original Don José in *Carmen* at the Opéra-Comique. Generally speaking, however, the performances were of a mediocre description.[1] The arrival and departure of débutants went on almost without intermission. An American procession gave noteworthy evidence of the new *embarras de choix* that Mapleson was enjoying. One recalls operas like *Faust* with Nordica, *Carmen* with Minnie Hauk, *Mireille* with Emma Nevada, *Martha* with Marie Engle; not to mention *Les Pêcheurs de Perles* with Alma Fohström and *La Favorita* with Hélène Hastreiter—all of them heard during this cheap " go as you please " season.

But the historic summer of 1887 was at hand. No one then dreamed of the renaissance that was on the way. The fate of opera in London at that juncture

---

[1] My impressions of the inaugural performance were thus recorded : "Evidence of hasty and incomplete preparation marked the opening performance of *La Traviata*. In fact, the only redeeming features, from an artistic point of view, were the very promising début of Mme Lillian Nordica, as Violetta, and the impersonation of the elder Germont by that reliable baritone, Signor Del Puente. The former is an American by birth and has a soprano voice of bright, clear, sympathetic timbre, admirably produced. It is of even quality and considerable power, notably in the head register. As a singer Mme Nordica possesses no slight agility, in addition to charm and purity of expression. As an actress her full capacity was not made apparent at the outset, but all her efforts were distinguished by intelligence and earnestness. Her reception was most favourable ".

literally hung in the balance.   Three or four companies
were in the field.   But the Gyes were out of it ; Mapleson had lost the confidence of the public ; and Lago
had never really succeeded in gaining it.   The Carl
Rosa Company, occupying Drury Lane in May,
naturally had only opera in English to offer; and
Society, at Covent Garden at least, would have none
of it.   Then, like a bolt from the blue, came Augustus
Harris with his brilliant four weeks' campaign, supported by a strong section of the aristocracy, led by
Lady de Grey and Lady Charles Beresford.   In the
unfolding of that revolutionary object-lesson several
first-rate artists, in addition to the brothers Jean and
Edouard de Reszke, were to play their parts ; and
among them was the new American soprano, Lillian
Nordica.

Her *rentrée* as Violetta on the second night of the
Drury Lane season (June 14th) was marked by an
innovation.   Instead of wearing the customary up-to-
date Paris costumes, she dressed the " Dame aux
Camélias " like the rest of the company, in the period of
Dumas' story.   When *Don Giovanni* was revived for
Maurel, her Donna Elvira revealed a well-trained
Mozart singer.   Her Marguerite derived a fresh charm
from association with a trio of such gifted men as Jean
de Reszke (Faust), Maurel (Valentine), and Edouard
de Reszke (Mephistopheles).

But, most striking of all, as an example of innate
talent and rapid artistic growth, was her assumption of
Valentina in *Les Huguenots*, also given in Italian with
the same group of singers.   This exacting character she
now undertook for the first time.   The critics were
taken by surprise.   So far her acting had not been her
strong point ; but now, in the *grand duo* of the fourth

act, with the great Polish tenor for her Raoul, Nordica rose to heights not previously scaled. In a word, she made manifest the qualities as a lyric actress that foreshadowed her Wagnerian triumphs of the years to come.

3

During the interval between the Mapleson and Harris seasons I had become personally acquainted with Mme Nordica. We had a mutual friend in Sebastian Schlesinger, the song-writer, who took me to see her one afternoon at her house in Gloucester Place. She gave the impression of being a delightful woman. One could not help but admire her unusually intelligent face, her wonderfully expressive eyes and sensitive mouth. Her manner was by turns serious, humorous, and lively; always interesting. She did not, like most singers, make a point of sparing her voice, but when speaking kept it raised without effort, yet entirely free from American nasality. (Mrs. Norton, her mother, who was rather deaf, took pains to inform me that she could " always hear every word Lillian said ".) She talked a great deal about her art, but very little about artists, being in that respect an exception to the ordinary run of *prime donne*.

The future of opera, with all its surprising developments, was still obscure. But, after her success at Drury Lane had become assured, she said to me : " I feel I must work harder than ever now. I would like to settle in London and go on studying as many new rôles as I can master. I know my voice is not yet under entire control. A singer should never be satisfied, but go on working, working all the time ".

That was to be her motto all through her career.

By nature intensely ambitious, she realized that her gifts were of the kind which industry and concentration alone would enable her to bring to maturity. By now, too, she had acquired patience as well, and the value of these qualities was soon to be demonstrated. The tasks which she set herself to conquer grew ever more exacting, yet without resulting in a single failure, excepting—common experience!—when she essayed the baffling rôle of Carmen. It did not suit her any better than it suited Adelina Patti.

The attempt to sing Carmen was Nordica's initial effort of the season of 1888—the first given by Augustus Harris at Covent Garden and the first of six successive seasons in which she took part under his management. It was the year of Melba's début; and, in addition, Albani and Ella Russell, Minnie Hauk and Sigrid Arnoldson, Fursch-Madi and Marguerite Macintyre were all available for leading rôles. The situation was not exactly pleasant for the American soprano, and she had foreseen as much when writing to me on Februrary 22 :

" All the papers have been saying that I have been ' retained ' for the season at Covent Garden. As a matter of fact, this is not correct. Of course the question of repertory and the giving of *exclusive* right of parts to certain artists is as important to me as to them. Therefore until I know what I am to sing, and how often, etc., I can come to no real conclusion with Mr. Harris ".

Like the good business woman she was, she nevertheless contrived to secure her share of the " plums ". She had sung Aïda at Drury Lane in the previous year, but less effectively than now. Her Valentina and Marguerite also showed a further advance ; while even as Selika in *L'Africaine*—another new part that, like Carmen, did not really lie well for her voice—she displayed to advantage her strong feeling for the picturesque.

4

Whilst strengthening her position as an operatic favourite, Nordica had also made her mark in oratorio. For that branch of the art disposition and training alike fitted her, and, had she so wished, it would have helped even more than opera to identify her permanently with English musical life. She was one of the soloists at the Handel Festival of 1888, distinguishing herself, on the Selection Day, by the remarkable power and bell-like quality of her head notes. I recall particularly her brilliant runs in the air " So shall the lute and harp ". She also sang at the Chester Musical Festival that summer; and thenceforward her services were for several years in regular demand at the great provincial gatherings as well as in London concert-rooms.

So far Nordica's work in opera had followed a well-beaten track. The season of 1889, when she was making her home in England, was marked by a new departure. Without knowing it, she opened up the most important chapter in her artistic career. I allude to her first appearance in Wagnerian opera. It had long been her desire to sing Elsa. Those, however, were still the days when people cherished the idea that the declamatory music of Wagner was calculated to ruin young voices; and certain of her English friends —her teacher (or " coach ") Alberto Randegger among them—had persistently dissuaded her from running the risk. She asked me what I thought. I had not held the same opinion and pointed to Albani, Rosa

Sucher, Lilli Lehmann, and other famous singers as examples to the contrary.

Then one day—it was whilst she was living in Fitzjohn's Avenue, Hampstead,—she informed me that she had succumbed to the wiles of Jean de Reszke (who was anxious for her to appear with him in *Lohengrin*) and had been studying Elsa in Italian. She was not destined, though, to attack the outlying forts of Bayreuth for the first time in Jean de Reszke's company. It was still early in the season of 1889, and the De Reszkes had not yet arrived in London from Paris, when Harris announced that he was going to mount *Lohengrin* for the Italian début of Barton McGuckin, the popular Irish tenor of the Carl Rosa Company.

The persuasive impresario required Nordica for the rôle of Elsa. He thought it would serve as a good public rehearsal for her performance with Jean. Half regretfully she consented; and then something else happened. McGuckin had the bad luck to sprain his ankle and was unable to go on. At the last moment another Lohengrin was found in Antonio d'Andrade (brother of a well-known baritone, Francesco d'Andrade), who was a new member of the company. So, on May 30th, with a Spaniard instead of an Irishman, and minus a full rehearsal with either, the new Elsa duly led her maidens to face Henry the Fowler on the banks of the Scheldt.

In spite of all these obstacles, she conquered. She made a handsome picture, notably in the scene of the bridal procession, where her regal gown, procured expressly from Germany, exceeded in sumptuousness any that had previously been seen here in the opera. But, what was more important, her rendering of the character revealed her powers in a new light. To quote words of my own :

" She invested it with rare sympathy and charm, and acted throughout with admirable intelligence. The music lay well within her means, and the fresh, bright quality of her voice enhanced the beauty of more than one familiar passage ". (*Musical Notes*, 1889.)

Still, this was only the beginning. The continuation came in America, where, in the autumn of the same year, Lillian Nordica made her first appearance at the Metropolitan Opera House. There in course of time Italian translations became discarded in favour of Wagner's original text. There, during a visit to New York in the spring of 1896, I heard Jean de Reszke and Nordica sing Lohengrin and Elsa in German ; and a great night it was for her. Apart from the artistic triumph, there was an enthusiastic ovation when she was presented on the stage (after the bridal duet) with a handsome diamond tiara subscribed for by a number of her millionaire friends and admirers.[1]

The gifted Anton Seidl conducted that performance, and it was to his admirable instruction, I was told, that the artist mainly owed the advance now discernible in her interpretation. Something, however, was also due to Cosima Wagner, with whom she had studied Venus in *Tannhäuser* at Bayreuth, where she had appeared as Elsa in 1894. Her German accent was now irre-

[1] We supped together after the performance, and, to compensate for my not being able to remain in New York to hear them together in *Tristan and Isolde* (I was booked to sail for Liverpool the following day), Mme Nordica and Jean de Reszke, forgetting their fatigue, sat up till the " early hours " in order to sing for me the love duet from the second act, with Amherst Webber at the piano.

proachable, and her declamatory skill, like her acting, had improved almost beyond recognition. It was, in fact, a period of steady, consistent progress along the right lines.

Seidl had also taught Nordica her Isolde. He was an extraordinary genius, no matter in what branch of his art he laboured; and in the New England singer he found splendid material for the exercise of his profound mastery of the Wagnerian répertoire. Her intense gratitude to him was openly and ungrudgingly expressed in a hundred ways.[1] Seidl conducted *Tristan* at Covent Garden in 1897, when Jean de Reszke made his first appearance there in that rôle; but Sedlmair, not Nordica, was then the Isolde. Not until June of the following year did I hear the two singers together in a German performance of Wagner's music-drama, and then it was a revelation on the part of both. We had now the ideal Tristan matched by an Isolde not merely versed in what were known as the Bayreuth traditions, but worthy to be compared with Ternina herself, who, only a fortnight before, had made her English début in the same character. The test was no light one, but the Transatlantic singer emerged from it triumphantly.

The final climax to Nordica's ascent of the Wagnerian peaks was reached when, in 1897, she sang for the first time at Covent Garden the Brünnhilde of *Siegfried* and *Götterdämmerung*, with Jean de Reszke for her companion in the former. By this time she had become so popular with the British public that her complete success in the most exacting of lyric rôles was hailed with all-round satisfaction. In New York

[1] See on this point Henry T. Finck's *Success in Music*, pp. 161–5.

her Brünnhilde was no less admired. She had had to wait a year, however, for the chance of playing the part there, because on the sudden death of Klafsky, who had been engaged for it, the exclusive " right " to the rôle had been claimed (in virtue of a clause in her contract) by no less a person than Mme Melba! Nordica had consequently not been engaged.[1]

But most welcome of all to the artist was the praise bestowed upon her Isolde by the severe German critics at the newly-opened Prinz-Regenten Theatre in Munich during the first Wagner Festival. She told me that she had been trembling in her shoes until the curtain fell on the first act. Then the enthusiasm of the audience had completely restored her confidence. So in twenty years, or thereabouts, the untrained girl whom I had first heard with a brass band at the Crystal Palace had risen to the topmost heights of her profession. She had won a position that not only brought honour to herself, but, as has been said, was to prove the " open sesame " for the ever-growing crowd of American opera singers who came after her.

5

So much for the artistic side of Nordica's romance.

[1] Krehbiel thus describes the incident : " It soon turned out that the failure to secure Mme Nordica was to cost the management dear. Mme Melba sang the part once, and so injured her voice that she had to retire for the season. . . . The manager's judgment was never at fault in these negotiations; he wanted to secure the services of Mme Nordica for he well knew their value, but the unhappy contract with Melba stood in his way, and Mme Nordica was beyond his reach when the failure of Melba's voice and her departure for France left the company crippled ". (*Chapters of Opera.*)

She had vowed to " get to the top ", and, possessing
all the requisite qualities, had done so. Unfortunately,
she failed to display equal wisdom in the conduct of
her domestic affairs. It was not her fault, one imagines,
that she was too impressionable. That would have
mattered less had she proved herself a better judge of
character where husbands were concerned,—that is to
say, after her " first " had so tragically disappeared with
his balloon and left her a fascinating widow at the age
of 24. Eight or ten years elapsed after that misfortune
before she began seriously to contemplate marrying
again.

Her choice then fell upon a Hungarian singer named
Zoltan Döme, who had come to London in 1891. He
had made something of a reputation by his effective
rendering of his native ditties at Marlborough House
and at select social gatherings. He also appeared at the
first series of Promenade Concerts given under Arditi
at Covent Garden in the September of that year. His
voice was at that time a baritone, but, fired by the
example of Jean de Reszke, he decided to have himself " converted " into a tenor, and devoted about
eight months to the process. It was not wholly successful. His organ sounded thin and metallic when,
by June, 1892, he had forced it up sufficiently to sing
the small part of Donner in *Das Rheingold* in Mahler's
memorable cycle of the *Ring* at Covent Garden. It
was his first step on the operatic ladder—and also his
last.

With this good-looking young fellow—careless of
money as he was of voice—Lillian Nordica promptly
fell in love, and he subsequently accompanied her to
America. Their marriage in 1896 was soon followed
by a divorce. When I went to live in New York at

the end of 1901, she was once more free, though commonly reported to be about to take a third husband. That final venture she did not make until later on. Meanwhile in 1902 she revisited London and sang at her last Covent Garden season.

During my lengthy sojourn in America our friendship grew closer as I learned to know her fine character better. I visited her frequently both in the city and at the country-place near Ossining rented by her from George W. Young, the banker, whom I met there. He was the man whom she afterwards married ; but the union, like her previous marital ventures, was not a happy one. Nor was her return to the New York boards fraught with unalloyed satisfaction for herself and her friends.

The redoubtable Oscar Hammerstein had engaged her for his second season (1907) at the Manhattan Opera House, and she opened it as the heroine of Ponchielli's *La Gioconda*, giving a superb performance of a rôle that was new to her repertory. But after a few appearances in that opera and *Aïda*, it became evident that Mr Hammerstein, for reasons of his own, was not particularly anxious for her to sing any more. Anyhow he tried to make things as unpleasant as he could for her.

Among the several devices he employed was one which she afterwards described as " smoking me out ". Knowing her objection to tobacco fumes, and being himself never without a cigar in his mouth (even on the stage, where he sat puffing through every performance), Hammerstein arranged for a " combined attack " during a matinée of *Aïda*, and, with the assistance of his conductor (Cleofonte Campanini), his régisseur (Coini), and an army of stage-carpenters,

created an atmosphere so thick, so noxious to his
prima donna, that she very nearly failed to get through
the opera. The last *entr'acte* was extended to a
smoky half hour, and an apology had to be made
to the audience. That sufficed for Hammerstein's
purpose. Mme Nordica was not called upon to sing
again during the remainder of the season.

6

At about the same period she became very interested
in the latest developments of the gramophone.
Unlike Mme Melba and Mme Sembrich, she had
never made any records, nor did she seem very
anxious to begin doing so. Her interest lay chiefly in
the educational direction, and one day she unfolded to
me a project for singing a series of exercises, to be
recorded as a model for imitation by vocal students.
She did not think the gramophone could be put to a
better use, and if I would undertake to prepare the
exercises she was ready to make records of them. I
talked the matter over with the Columbia Graphophone
Company and arranged a contract with them; I
devoted my spare time for several months to inventing
and writing a long series of exercises, filling 10 discs,
to be sung in different keys by contralto, tenor, and
bass voices, as well as by the soprano. But these last,
as it happened, were not to be recorded by the
originator of the scheme.

For, in spite of numerous tests and experiments
at the Columbia *atelier*, Mme Nordica, fettered by the
awkward conditions under which record-making then
laboured, found the work both strenuous and disappointing. She tried her hardest and sang her best;

but somehow the results were never, or rarely ever, quite satisfying. Once when she was away on tour she wrote me this letter:

LYNCHBURG,
VIRGINIA.
May 15th, 1908.

MY DEAR FRIEND,

At last I take the time to send you a line. Forgive me that I did not see more of you during my four days at home, but I simply could not.

When I get back, May 24th or 25th, I shall as soon as possible make a thorough trial for records. At present I am terribly discouraged about them. Still, I'll try once more and do my very best—but, for some reason I do not seem to have any success with them. There is not one which I or my family think fit to put before the public.

Of all I think the first half of " Tacea la notte " the best. Ah! well, I'll try again; perhaps I'll be more successful. . . . And believe me ever

Your sincere but procrastinating friend,
LILLIAN NORDICA.

Her " Suicidio ! " (*La Gioconda*) was, in my opinion, the best of all her attempts; but alas, she never achieved a record that was truly worthy of her or that conveyed the thrill of her beautiful tone. Her share in the educational scheme (or " Phono-vocal Method " as we christened it) was consequently abandoned. But I carried it to an issue on my own account, and, in the U.S.A. at least, it proved for a time fairly successful. Then the Columbia Co. lost interest in it, both there and in England, and in course of a few years what might have been a valuable aid alike to the teacher and the student of singing, gradually faded out of recollection.

During the latter portion of her career Mme

Nordica became an exceptionally fine singer of Lieder, employing her vocal gifts here, as she did in oratorio, not merely to dramatic ends alone, but for the attainment of poetic and refined expression, allied to artistic intelligence of a high order. There was in her tones a delightful variety of colour. She was one of the few women whom I have heard sing Schubert's " Erl-King " with the requisite differentiation of timbre for depicting all three characters—the father, the child, and the Erl-king.[1]

The catastrophe that prematurely ended her life was doubly tragic because it struck her down whilst she was still at the height of her powers. Happy in her matrimonial ventures she certainly had not been; and maybe she was welcoming the chance of forgetting her domestic troubles when she undertook, in 1914, a concert tour of the world. All went well until the month of April, when the s.s. *Tasmin*, by which she was travelling in Eastern waters, got wrecked off the coast of Java. During the prolonged rescue she suffered severe exposure, and this brought on an illness from which she died at Batavia on May 10th, just two days before her 55th birthday. In that far distant land, *requiescat in pace !*

---

[1] The German critic, A. Ehrlich, wrote of her in 1895, after her " extraordinary performance " in the *Traviata*, these words :
" Sovereign command of her music, finely-executed vocal *nuances*, an exquisitely delicate pianissimo, brilliant technique, soulful animation, a faultless art of phrasing and declamation and grace of delivery—all these are so many epithets which unprejudiced criticism can justly greet her with ". (*Berühmte Sängerinnen*, Leipzig.)
. Such tributes as this, and many besides, she was still evoking from the critics of her own country down to the end of the concert and recital period which closed her labours there.

x

CHAPTER X

THREE LATE-VICTORIANS

MUCH more to be envied than they imagined were the *fin-de-siècle* opera-lovers of the Victorian era. As will have been indicated by the preceding chapter, the smouldering embers of their one-time passion for Italian Opera had been fanned anew into flame through the enterprise of Sir Augustus Harris, backed up by Society's new leaders, Lady de Grey and Lady Charles Beresford, and countenanced by no less a personage than the popular Prince of Wales—later on King Edward VII. The interregnum, if such it really were, had lasted no more than a year or two. The Gyes and Mapleson, after nearly three decades of struggle and competition, had reached the end of their tether.

But the death of Tietjens and the retirement, partial or complete, of Patti, Nilsson, Lucca, and other stars of the first magnitude, by no means implied that the chain of great *cantatrices* had definitely snapped. On the contrary, such was the plethora of talent of the highest order forthcoming in the vocal world of those days, that the new links had been forming even whilst the old were growing thinner. Certain distinguished singers, whom the very brilliancy of those in the foremost rank had forced ever so slightly into the background, now stepped indisputably to the front, thus making room for newcomers equally gifted, who were in their turn to become the favourite *prime donne* of the hour.

Still active on the soprano list was Emma Albani, for we may be sure that Harris did not ignore her claims. Neither did he overlook those of Minnie Hauk, Sigrid Arnoldson, Ella Russell, Fursch-Madi, Zélie de Lussan, and others well known to the public, including famous contraltos like Trebelli, Scalchi, and Giulia Ravogli. Some of these already have or soon will have their place in these pages, in virtue of gifts that entitle them thereto. Marcella Sembrich, the great Polish *coloratura* singer, actually dated back to the Gye régime of 1880, but only now joins Nellie Melba and Emma Calvé (both introduced at Covent Garden by Harris) because it so happens that when this book is being written all three of these celebrated singers are still living.

I. MARCELLA SEMBRICH

I

When Henry E. Krehbiel first heard Sembrich, he wrote in the *New York Tribune* that " her voice wakened echoes of Mme Patti's organ, but has warmer life-blood in it " ; and the remark was quoted with approval by Henry T. Finck in his *Success in Music*. Personally I could never have shared their opinion. If there was one quality more than another in Patti's voice that invariably stimulated the admiration and delight of the listener, it was its rich full Italian warmth—a warmth, vibrant with luscious, penetrating volume, such as we are accustomed to associate with the song of the nightingale.

The resemblance between the voices of Patti and Sembrich pointed out by Krehbiel lay not so much in actual timbre as in an identical mechanical method, coupled with tonal features that were the outcome of a certain amount of imitation, conscious or unconscious, on Sembrich's part. For the *diva* had no more whole-hearted " heroine-worshipper " than little Marcella, who sang with her at Covent Garden for three consecutive seasons. " There is no one in the world ", she would say, " to be compared with Patti ; nor do I think there has ever been a singer exactly like her. We have all had to work hard to accomplish the things that she did with ridiculous ease ".

Sembrich's early life-story had been a veritable

To Mr. Herman : Klein
in kind remembrance of

Marcella Sembrich

romance. Born at Wisnewczyk, in Galicia (then Austrian Poland), on February 15, 1858, she breathed from the outset the atmosphere of music. Her father, Kasimir Kochanska, was a professional violinist, and from the time she was six he taught her his instrument. He had a family of nine sons and four daughters to bring up—until their musical abilities enabled them to support themselves by travelling about the country and playing together at fairs, weddings, etc. The future prima donna began ere long to evince a greater liking for the piano than the violin. Through the help of a wealthy friend, she was sent to the Conservatorium at Lemberg, and there she studied the instrument of her choice under a professor named Wilhelm Stengel, who in course of time was to become her husband.

Having worked with Stengel for about five years and grown into a remarkably good pianist, he took her to Vienna. There she obtained an audition from Professor Epstein, and sang for him as well. He was greatly impressed (albeit as a vocalist she was practically untrained), and advised her to give up the piano and study singing with Victor Rokitansky. After twelve months with Rokitansky, she went on to Milan—being now nearly eighteen—and for a couple of years worked under the younger Lamperti, son of the teacher of most of the distinguished sopranos then shining as operatic stars.

2

In 1877 she was pronounced ready for her début. Accordingly, Marcella assumed her mother's maiden name of Sembrich, and on June 3rd made her first appearance at Athens in Bellini's *I Puritani*. Success only served to stimulate her ambition to master German as well as Italian rôles. In order to do this, being now married to the devoted Stengel, she returned to Vienna and there worked under an experienced "coach". The result was an engagement in October, 1878, for the Hoftheater at Dresden, where she remained for a year and a half, adding substantially to her reputation and constantly improving her vocal and dramatic technique.

By the spring of 1880 her fame as a *coloratura* soprano had begun to reach London. English visitors to the Lower Rhine Festival that year had come back full of praises concerning a new soprano who had taken part in some of the concerts. Still, the name of Sembrich was not among the artists promised in the prospectus of the Covent Garden season. It was quite unexpectedly, therefore, that the critics found themselves invited to witness, on June 12th, her first appearance as Lucia. Most agreeable was the surprise in store for them, for they quickly perceived that they were listening to a singer upon whom the imminent risk of comparisons with an Adelina Patti or an Albani seemed to cast no noticeable shade. On the contrary, she shone so brilliantly that at the end of the season we find James Davison, of *The Times*, declaring that " Mr. Gye had even been fortunate enough to discover in Madame Sembrich a third star of all but equal brightness and power of attraction with those already named ".[1]

---

[1] The critic of *The Standard* wrote the following : " Madame Sembrich's début as Lucia created someting in the nature of a *furore*, and next morning the advent of a great artist was announced by the critics. . . . Her second appearance was as

These praises and predictions were to be amply verified during the next four seasons. It is interesting, however, to observe that even thus early, at the very beginning of her visits to England, she was demonstrating in the concert-room the exceptionally broad, versatile nature of her talent. I recollect particularly her introducing two *Lieder* at Sir Julius Benedict's annual concert in the Floral Hall (now the potato market) at Covent Garden. It was an absolute innovation, because at that time no prima donna ever dreamed of singing Schubert or Schumann, unless perhaps at a Philharmonic Concert.

3

Sembrich's voice at this period was singularly entrancing. I was immensely struck with the vibrant quality and bell-like purity of her tone, her impeccable intonation, and the faultless accuracy of her scales. She had a perfect shake, and the masterful ease and facility of her execution was displayed over a compass extending to the F in *alt*.

Her daring essay as Dinorah in 1881 was amusingly commented upon. Most of the critics found it hard to accept her in a part that brought her into immediate antagonism with the two greatest living interpreters of

successful as her first, and if expectations were slightly disappointed by her Amina, it was for the reason that her good qualities had unduly excited anticipation. She repeated Amina with the most satisfactory results, and won her way still further into the regard of audiences by her marvellously brilliant singing as the Queen in *Les Huguenots*. But brilliance is not her only strong point, as those know who heard the charming simplicity and feeling with which she lately sang some German *Lieder* at Sir Julius Benedict's concert ", the rôle—both then actually singing it in London—namely, Patti and Ilma di Murska. The fact remains, however, that she triumphed, in spite of a cold which had caused one postponement of the opera. She began only moderately well, her voice sounding rather weak and uncertain in the caressing melody of the *berceuse*, " Si, carina ". But with the Shadow Song " her powers returned, and her brilliant delivery of it roused an exceptionally apathetic audience to enthusiasm ". Marcella Sembrich was to conquer in similar fashion in other parts and in the face of tremendous rivalry.

Her Constanze in a revival of Mozart's *Seraglio* revealed the musician whose intimate mastery of the piano and violin helped to make her an ideal Mozart singer. In 1882 there was to contend with the " added glory " of Pauline Lucca, but that did not stand in Marcella's way. Whilst the former renewed an old triumph as Selika in *L'Africaine*, the younger artist achieved a new one with her superb Queen of Night in Mozart's *Flauto Magico*—a success won almost in the very presence of Ilma di Murska, the greatest Astrifiammente of her time !

The Gye régime at Covent Garden was now approaching its end. Nevertheless, in course of its last two seasons most of the old " stars " were pursuing their customary orbit ; and among them was the now-popular Mme Sembrich, singing better than ever. Her display of *l'audace, toujours l'audace*, was rewarded by equal success when she ventured to attack Caterina in *L'Etoile du Nord*, a difficult character undertaken ever since 1866 by no one save Adelina Patti. When she resumed this part in the following year, with Edouard de Reszke in Faure's favourite rôle of Peter the Great, the critics were of opinion that her impersonation had "undergone considerable improvement"; that it was "riper and fuller in its histrionic details"; and that "her singing was from first to last admirable in its refinement, correctness, and brilliancy".

4

Meanwhile Marcella Sembrich had appeared at the Metropolitan Opera House, New York, under the management of Henry E. Abbey, on the second night of his opening season at the new theatre, October 24th, 1883. This "memorable event", as Krehbiel rightly termed it (having regard to subsequent musical history in the United States), may be said to have prolonged the inaugural celebrations. They had been started two nights before with a performance of Gounod's *Faust* in which Christine Nilsson, Scalchi, and Campanini sang, and there was lively curiosity to hear Sembrich, whose high European reputation had preceded her. Not for a moment was her success in doubt. Opera-lovers instantly took her to their hearts and have held her there ever since.

She subsequently gave a Protean display of versatility at Henry Abbey's benefit concert, when she sang an aria, contributed a violin obbligato for Christine Nilsson, and played a Chopin mazurka upon the piano for an encore. During that season she made amazing headway in New York, and the critics waxed eloquent over the archness and sprightliness of her acting, apart from the elegance and grace of her singing in two of Patti's greatest rôles, Rosina in *Il Barbiere* and Zerlina in *Don Giovanni*. Yet, notwithstanding this splendid introduction, fifteen years were to elapse before she sang again at the Metropolitan.

Meanwhile, in the summer of 1883, her first proceeding, after leaving London, was to go to Milan and place herself under the *elder* Lamperti for a supplemental period of strict vocal training! It was a wise, courageous course to pursue, and it had its reward in the years that followed, when she was by degrees ripening into one of the finest Lieder-singers of her time. Sembrich was never too proud to receive instruction. She once told me that one of her chief pleasures,—when she crossed the ocean to take her annual holiday in the Swiss mountains and stay for a couple of months at her favourite spot, Karersee, in the Dolomites,—was to "meet her old teacher and take a few lessons in singing".

Modesty, entire freedom from conceit, has always been a predominant characteristic of this great artist's nature. If it had been possible for her to be "spoilt", America would have spoiled her long ago. When she went back to the Metropolitan in 1898 it was to establish a supremacy in her particular line of parts that lasted unchallenged until her retirement eleven years later. Retaining her youth and freshness in the most marvellous way, her art seemed to acquire greater finish, greater charm, greater *maestria* as time went on. She it was who did more than any other singer to keep alive in a Wagner-ridden community the popularity of the florid old Italian operas.

With the song-recitals which she gave regularly in New York and the leading Eastern cities she achieved more than monetary gain. She educated her public in the appreciation of a very wide range of classics and the gems of the great Lieder-writers, from

Schubert, Schumann, and Brahms down to Wolf and Strauss. It was always a welcome sight to see the eager crowd that filled Carnegie Hall whenever she gave a recital, to hear the thunders of applause as she tripped on or off the platform. The exquisitely musical quality of her voice enabled it to penetrate easily to the farthest corners of that huge place; and one could perceive and enjoy without effort every delicate *nuance*, every agile ornament that enriched her song. No style, no school came amiss to her.

But it was as a Mozart singer that, to the writer, she appealed most of all; for she combined in herself all the superlative gifts that go to the making of that rare phenomenon. Nor would the ordinary spectator have ever guessed how greatly her outward calmness belied her. She was, she confessed, a " bundle of nerves ", and was so short-sighted that without her *lorgnette* she could not distinguish people or objects a couple of yards in front of her. How she managed on the stage she hardly knew, but apparently the difficulty made no difference to her art.

I only saw Sembrich once in a rôle in which she did not seem thoroughly at home. The opera was Paderewski's *Manru*, which, after obtaining a favourable reception at Dresden, Zurich, Cologne, and elsewhere in 1901, was given at the New York Metropolitan in February, 1902. The composer was present, and there was much acclamation; but the opera, based upon a stupid story and musically rather monotonous, proved the failure that it deserved to be. Sembrich seldom made mistakes, and had it not been to please her illustrious countryman she would never, probably, have undertaken the part of the heroine.

The night of February 6th, 1909, when Marcella

Sembrich took formal leave of the stage at the Metropolitan Opera House, was marked by a deeper sense of emotion and personal affection than is usually to be observed on occasions of the kind. I sat beside her husband, dear old Wilhelm Stengel, who had invited me to accompany him to his wife's "farewell". He sat silently weeping most of the evening, but it cheered him up somewhat when he went behind after each scene from an opera (*Don Pasquale*, the *Barber*, and *Traviata*) to embrace his "Marzelline", and help her to pile up the huge floral emblems that were handed over the footlights. Three months later I bade the Stengel-Sembrichs a hearty adieu on returning to live in my native country, where I heard later on of the death of the teacher and husband whose companionship and wise counsel had been so precious to this gifted woman. After that event she ceased to give recitals or appear at concerts, and occupied herself with teaching the rising generation in the cities of New York and Philadelphia.

II. NELLIE MELBA

I am one of the few living persons—certainly the only English writer on musical subjects—who happened to hear Dame Melba sing at Princes' Hall, Piccadilly, in 1886, when she was still Mrs Nellie Armstrong, of Melbourne, New South Wales. Remembering well what an untrained vocalist she then was and the lovely natural quality of her voice, I can give full credit to Mme Mathilde Marchesi for the improvement which was manifest in the singer's style on her return to London two years later.

The clever old teacher had been wise enough, where the production of tone was involved, to "let well alone". She had seen at once that in this case it would be impossible to better the work of nature. She did not even attempt to darken the rather white timbre of the medium register, but left it bright, silvery, glistening, just as she had found it. Instead of paying attention to that, she cultivated without forcing the head notes in her own characteristic, Garcia-like way. She extended their tessitura without converting the musical *soprano leggiero* into a *soprano sfogato*. She taught her pupil a perfect scale and a delicious shake, and made of her a facile, flexible, brilliant vocalist.

It was a quick transformation. In little more than a year after Melba had begun study with Marchesi in

Paris she was ready to make her début in opera. One or two of the French critics had heard her at semi-private concerts, and wrote only simple truth when they declared her to be one of those rare beings who sang like the birds—" comme le rossignol ". Yet Paris was not to be the scene of her earliest successes. It was from the Théâtre de la Monnaie, at Brussels, that the news of her extraordinary triumph as Gilda in *Rigoletto* (October 12, 1887) was trumpeted forth to the world. As her teacher, who was present, said in her book (*Marchesi and Music*), " The very next day and afterwards it was nothing but a chorus of praise everywhere; the entire press of Brussels declaring the young *artiste* to be a star of the first magnitude ".

She was now known as " Melba " ; and the reports of her success had speedily reached Augustus Harris. That rising impresario had taken no interest whatever in her when she first visited London and sought to secure an engagement with him. British opera-goers still remained unmoved by the advent of an Australian soprano who had been creating excitement across the Channel. They refused to flock in crowds to Covent Garden to witness her first appearance there on Queen Victoria's birthday, May 24th, 1888. The audience was a large and fashionable one, certainly ; and a great deal was expected of the débutante by the habitués who had heard and read reports about her. But the critics, accustomed to take such things *cum grano salis*, assumed their usual calm, judicial attitude and, what is more, preserved it until they had written their notices. The latter were careful without being enthusiastic.

The opera was *Lucia di Lammermoor*. It progressed

for the best part of two acts "without incident".
Nor was it until after the Mad Scene that the house
began to wake up and indulge in warm applause or
displays amounting finally to what is termed an
ovation. The sextet went well, however, and was
cordially received. My own impressions were of a
mingled description. I found the amateur had given
place to the artist; I thought the quality of her voice
was exceptionally beautiful; but, on the whole, the
singer left me cold.[1]

With this opinion the general verdict was in full
agreement, even though not expressed on all hands
with the same frankness. On the other hand, Mme
Melba succeeded instantly in winning the suffrages of
Society. She made more friends among the wealthy
patrons of the "Royal Italian Opera" than any new
prima donna of that period, whatever her nationality.
These friendships, which she never failed to foster
and utilize, were to stand her in good stead all

---

[1] This is how I summed up the Australian singer after the
season had terminated:

"Mme Melba possesses a flexible high soprano voice of
resonant timbre and extensive compass; her means are under
perfect control and her vocalization is of a brilliant order.
There can be no doubt that her powers as a singer are above
the average; at the same time her style, judged from the loftiest
standpoint, is disfigured by certain mannerisms and to an extent
deficient in that indescribable something which we call charm.
Her *tours de force* are dazzling enough, but her accents lack the
ring of true pathos; she sings and acts with admirable intelligence, but in both the gift of spontaneous feeling is denied her.
This definition is essential in order to explain how it was that
Mme Melba, despite the warm reception accorded her at the
outset, failed to maintain the advantage she had gained and
establish herself among reigning operatic favourites." (*Musical
Notes*, 1888.)

through the only difficult or uphill portion of her career.

2

But more valuable by far, in an artistic sense, to one who was still comparatively a stage novice, was the practical advice that she received from the famous Polish tenor who was her constant associate during her second season at Covent Garden. Then it was that she really began to master certain fundamental principles of her art of which she had previously commanded little more than a smattering. From him she acquired the old Italian system of breathing, which Mme Marchesi too frequently allowed her pupils to pick up as best they could. Until that time Melba had been a vocalist *et praterea nihil.* Jean de Reszke practically taught her how to act, how to impart ease and significance to her gestures, how to move about the stage with grace and dignity.

Jean de Reszke had sung in Gounod's opera for the first time in Paris during the previous winter (1888–89), with Adelina Patti, when *Roméo et Juliette* was transferred from the Opéra-Comique to the Opéra. I had had the good fortune to be present at that historic *première,* and was able to make comparisons. I knew full well that the glamour, the excitement, the amazing " atmosphere " of that night could never be recaptured, either at Covent Garden or at any other opera-house. But a Roméo such as Jean de Reszke must perforce inspire any Juliette, however inexperienced, however unequal to him in dramatic calibre. And so it proved. He and Melba had rehearsed together with such sedulous care that not a tiny point in their stage business was overlooked. So perfectly did their voices blend, so faultless was their intonation, so identical their phrasing, that the long series of duets proved a joy from first to last.

Looking back now upon this interesting event, I cannot help thinking that the advance which it showed touched in many respects the high water-mark of Dame Melba's achievement as a lyric artist. She may have essayed more exacting parts—some that did not suit her at all; only one or two that fitted her quite so well. But no one save Patti ever sang Juliette's waltz-air with the same extraordinary ease, with the same *insouciance* (there is no English word for it), or the same pearl-like clarity of execution in *appoggiature*, runs, and cadenzas.

Because he inspired her, Melba always appeared to greater advantage with Jean de Reszke than with any other tenor. When he was the Faust her acting in the Garden and Prison scenes would wax warmer and even a trace of passion might glow in her silvery tones. In less familiar music the incandescence would be missing. It was so in Goring Thomas's *Esmeralda* (given at Covent Garden in French in 1890), when she sang the title-rôle to Jean's Captain Phœbus ; and in Bemberg's new opera *Elaine* (1892). Yet even when the vital spark was lacking, its absence could be overlooked in the enjoyment of Melba's " glorious medium " (so Jean de Reszke used to describe it), the exquisite *coloratura*, the facile flow of girlish and delicate yet vibrant head tone. Hence could one delight in her " Caro nome ", her " Jewel Song ", her Mad Scene in *Hamlet*, her " Willow Song " in Verdi's *Otello*.

3

The ambition to sing heavier rôles led her now and again to essay tasks that lay physically beyond her. She should never, for instance, have attempted Wagner. Her first venture in that direction was at the Paris Opéra, where, so early as '90 or '91, she sang Elsa to the Lohengrin of Ernest van Dyck. A few months later she undertook the part at Covent Garden, struggling through the opening act under an attack of nervousness that nearly upset her. In the duet with Ortrud she plucked up courage somewhat, and in the wedding scene she wore a cloth-of-gold gown that dazzled all beholders. But, on the whole, her voice was naturally too light for the music of Elsa; she was unable to cope with its declamatory needs. Her experiment as Brünnhilde in *Siegfried* came near to injuring her voice permanently. That, however, did not happen in London but in New York.

Dame Melba's legitimate triumphs were won in those less exacting rôles which really lay within her means. One of the best of these was Nedda, a part that she took when *Pagliacci* was first produced at Covent Garden in May, 1893. Leoncavallo—not, as a rule, a particularly demonstrative Italian—went into such raptures over her delicious rendering of the *ballatella* that, after leading the demand for a repetition, he could not forbear rushing behind forthwith to embrace her before the end of the act. In the second tableau Melba acted with a spirit and *entrain* very rare with her, and sang magnificently. The excitement of the scene allowed full scope for her dramatic idea, which was to present Columbine as a kind of second-rate provincial actress. Altogether it provided a vivid realization of Leoncavallo's conception.

Melba's Nedda in a sense foreshadowed her yet more popular embodiment of Mimi in *La Bohème*, which was not seen, however, until six years later. She had in the meantime added to her repertory such important characters as Violetta, Micaela, Rosina in *Il Barbiere*, and the Queen in *Les Huguenots;* while in 1904 she created at Covent Garden the heroine of a short opera entitled *Hélène*, which was written expressly for her by Saint-Saëns.

But in none of these parts did she make the same strong impression as in Puccini's early opera. The earnest, sentimental nature of the devoted *grisette* appealed to her strongly, and the music, at once straightforward, melodious, and touching, brought out all that was sweetest and purest in the voice of the Australian singer. No wonder she repeated here the hit that she had made in the part with the same Musetta (Zélie de Lussan) in America the previous year. It was in scenes from *La Bohème* that Dame Melba last appeared upon the stage of Covent Garden when she bade her operatic farewell to the British public in the summer of 1926.

Thirty-eight years is a lengthy span for the career of an opera singer. Few have equalled and still fewer have exceeded it. Stamina, not age, is the test in these cases; and if Melba's voice retained its silvery timbre and resonance for a period beyond the common, it was the result of her exceptionally unartificial, effortless method of producing it. For the same reason, coupled with the amazing ease that marked her execution of the most difficult *tours de force*, her singing never failed to give the listener unalloyed pleasure.

Hence the fact that she became one of the most popular artists of her day.

Among the things that contributed substantially to her fortune was the gramophone, of whose potentialities she was perhaps the first singer to be a successful and profitable exponent.

III. EMMA CALVÉ

I

" A troublesome creature, decidedly ", Augustus Harris was wont to declare, " but well worth all the trouble she gives. As a woman she is wilful, capricious, rather bad-tempered. As an artist she always wants her own way ; but, once she has got it, you can rely upon her doing the most splendid things imaginable, and working her hardest to secure an all-round success ".

Sir Augustus, although diplomatic, was rather too easy-going in his dealings with singers, and he had hesitated considerably before engaging Calvé for Covent Garden, because he had heard that she was difficult to manage. However, after her extraordinary success as Santuzza at the Opéra-Comique in Paris in January, 1892, he could no longer hesitate. Whether troublesome or not, here was the ideal heroine for his first production of *Cavalleria Rusticana*. It had only been done in London by a scratch Italian company,[1] the opera being then barely eighteen months old.

Emma Calvé had no difficulty in surpassing her rivals of the period in this particular rôle; for it fitted her to absolute perfection. The original Santuzza, Gemma Bellincioni, who was to play it in London three years later, acted much better than she sang. Calvé seemed to bring into the opera the

[1] At the Shaftesbury Theatre under Signor Lago during the autumn of 1891.

Sicilian atmosphere of Verga's story, just as Duse had brought it into the drama. The wonderful sunlit *mise en scène*, the strong *couleur locale* provided by Harris did the rest. It was equivalent to seeing and hearing Sonzogno's prize work for the first time. *Cavalleria Rusticana* had been running like wild-fire through the capitals of Europe; the name of the new composer, Pietro Mascagni, was on every lip; Queen Victoria had " commanded " a performance by Lago's company at Windsor Castle a few months before.

Unforgettable, then, was the impression made on May 16th, by the first *real* Santuzza, when she emerged from a hot, dusty lane into the burning sunshine of the village market-square. Gliding covertly, restlessly, in search of her missing lover; glancing from side to side with anxious face; her fingers pulling at her Sicilian shawl, as ever and anon she slipped it off and replaced it on her shoulders—she looked a veritable picture of abject, hopeless misery. Then for the first time we heard the poignant tones of Calvé's penetrating yet round, ringing, sympathetic voice. It seemed to have the sombre quality of a contralto miraculously impinged upon the acute timbre and high range of a soprano—the best voice of all for the expression of mental anguish, suffering, pleading, and despair. The sordid story told to Mamma Lucia in the *romanza* held a heightened force, touching a thousand hearts besides that of Turiddu's mother; creating the sure conviction that beneath the humble exterior of the Italian peasant-girl were working the mind and the genius of a born tragic actress.[1]

[1] As an appreciation of Calvé at this interesting period of her career, I reproduce the criticism which described her début on May 16th, 1892, in the *Sunday Times :* " Mme Calvé sheds

CALVÉ AS CARMEN

During that season, between May and July, she sang on no fewer than twenty-two occasions. The public consistently flocked to hear her, notwithstanding a torrent of competing operatic attractions the like of which, for quality no less than quantity, London has never experienced.[1] The immediate outcome of her success was an offer from Abbey and Grau of £20,000 for a ten months' tour in the United States. To accept this necessitated her breaking her contract with

new light upon the character of Santuzza. Others have depicted well enough the sufferings of the poor girl; but it has remained for Mme Calvé to bring out the true dog-like nature of this pitiable creature; to express by look and gesture her sense of utter helplessness; to fill in the picture with a hundred little artistic touches that tell the story where the librettist and musician cannot. It is a study from the life. Watch her attitude as she recounts her sad tale to Mamma Lucia; note her shrug of the shoulders as she sits, arms akimbo, pretending not to hear the taunts of Lola; observe her gestures of anger, defiance, affection, pleading, and despair as she struggles for love and kindness with Turiddu. She is a Sicilian to the finger-tips.

" But besides being a superb actress Mme Calvé is a remarkably fine singer. Her voice, still fresh and unimpaired by hard work, is one of those expressive organs that can convey a given emotion without the aid of language. Her command of tone-colour is extraordinary; there are moments when the power and intensity of her notes thrill one to the core. The timbre is wonderfully bright and resonant, the character of the voice essentially dramatic, and from top to bottom of the scale there is not a trace of *vibrato* ".

[1] In 1892 Sir Augustus Harris gave grand opera at Drury Lane as well as at Covent Garden, filling both houses regularly with crowded audiences at high prices. Mahler conducted the German; Mancinelli, Bevignani, and Randegger the Italian and French representations. The combined companies consisted of 75 artists; 25 operas were mounted in ten weeks, three of them novelties. The leading singers comprised nearly all the European celebrities of the day.

M. Carvalho to return to the Opéra-Comique. But a hurried visit to Paris and a *solatium* of £2,000 soon procured the desired " leave " ; and in due time Mme Calvé discovered a new El Dorado under the auspices of her American managers.

2

She was born in 1864 at Decazeville in the department of Aveyron, situated in the south of France.[1] Her voice having attracted notice, her mother took her to Paris, and there she studied for two years under Puget, a former operatic tenor. At Nice in 1881 she took part in a charity performance, but her professional life dates actually from September 23, 1882, when she appeared at the Théâtre de la Monnaie, Brussels, as Marguerite in *Faust*.

Nothwithstanding a favourable reception, the keen ear of M. Gevaert, the director of the Brussels Conservatoire, detected certain defects in her technique. Accordingly, he sent her to Mme Marchesi, under whom she completed her vocal education. At the end of 1884 she was engaged for the Théâtre-Italien in Paris, where she created the part of Alfaïma in a new opera by Theodore Dubois, entitled *Aben-Hamet*, with Victor Maurel and Edouard de Reszke for her chief companions. She quickly became a favourite and was engaged shortly afterwards for the Opéra-Comique, where she made a brilliant début on March 11th, 1885, as Hélène in Joncières' opera, *Le Chevalier Jean*.

[1] Her *family name* was given by M. Jules Martin in the *Annuaire des Planches* for 1895 as " Emma de Roquer ", and at that date she was living at Paris in the Avenue Montaigne.

She soon proved herself a good Mozart singer by her performances as the Countess in *Figaro* and Pamina in the *Magic Flute*. Then, in the winter of 1886–7 she proceeded to Milan, and at La Scala sang (under Sonzogno's directorate) the principal part in *Flora Mirabilis*, an opera by a Greek composer, Spiro Samara; besides appearing as Leila in Bizet's *Pêcheurs de Perles* and as Ophélie in Thomas's *Hamlet*. This engagement indicates the date of her first association with the famous Milanese publisher who was subsequently to discover Mascagni and to give the world *Cavalleria Rusticana*. Gemma Bellincioni had naturally had a considerable start with Santuzza in Italy; but she found a dangerous rival in Emma Calvé, whose triumphs in the part elsewhere decided M. Carvalho to engage her to create it in French at the Opéra-Comique. She did so on January 19th, 1892, and in the following May went on to set the seal upon her fame in Mascagni's opera at Covent Garden.

Even more noteworthy, however, was her dazzling London success as Carmen.[1] She spent a considerable time in Spain for the purpose of acquiring the right local colour. Yet when she essayed Carmen at the Opéra-Comique, her impersonation proved altogether too Spanish for the liking of the Parisians, who had been accustomed to the essentially French conception of the original—Mme Galli-Marié. Then she made her appearance in the part at Covent Garden, and with it took London by storm. Here it was pronounced

[1] New York, a few months later, duplicated those triumphs with compound interest; but a curious diversity of critical opinion was manifested there regarding the respective merits of her Carmen and her Santuzza.

without hesitation to be the ideal Carmen, not a single dissentient voice being heard.

Six months later Calvé made a memorable début at the Metropolitan Opera House as Santuzza, and followed it up with an even more overwhelming success in *Carmen*. Nothing like the rush to hear her in Bizet's opera had been experienced in New York since the final stages of the Patti "craze". And yet the opinions of the critics showed a curious tendency to pick holes in her performance. Krehbiel went so far as to complain that the new Carmen had become "so much of a mere fad that the public remained all but insensible to the merits of her immeasurably finer impersonation of Santuzza". And so forth and so on.

3

But there are many rôles besides these outstanding ones of Carmen and Santuzza to which the singer lent distinction and interest. Gifted as she was with imagination and versatility, with a voice of the most accommodating range, and with genuine dramatic power, she took a pride in inventing new "business" for the older parts as well as for those which she created. Thus, her Marguerite, her Ophélie, her Margherita in *Mefistofele*, her Leila in *Les Pêcheurs de Perles*, her Messaline in De Lara's opera of that name, were treated with the utmost originality. Each of her new creations in turn presented vivid and striking features, to be remembered because in course of time they became traditional.

In the early days we also saw her in two such widely-contrasted characters as Suzel in Mascagni's *L'Amico Fritz* (1892) and Massenet's *La Navarraise*

(1894)—the former all simplicity and grace; the latter the heroine of a tale of bloodshed, who passes through a rapid nightmare of horrors. Her Sapho (1897) was never seen here, but Paris placed it with her Navarraise and her Santuzza at the very pinnacle of her achievements. Massenet called her the " incomparable tragedian-singer ", and a famous French critic wrote : " She is a thinker, a seeker, much more than an instinctive artist; she lives all her rôles beforehand by thinking them deeply ". Including Lalla Rookh (Félicien David), and the various characters named in course of this sketch, her whole répertoire totalled over twenty parts.

Her ultimate addition thereto was made in 1904 towards the close of her final season at Covent Garden. She then appeared as the heroine in Massenet's *Hérodiade*, or rather in a mutilated version of that opera performed under the title of *Salomé*. She bade farewell to the stage in 1910, but came to England no more, save very rarely for a private visit to her faithful friend Mme Guy d'Hardelot. Continuing to make her home in Paris, she also occasionally appeared at a few concerts before admiring crowds in the United States. " A little work ", she said, " helps me to keep young ".

CHAPTER XI

SOME CELEBRATED CONTRALTOS

I. MARIETTA ALBONI

I

I DID not have the luck to hear Marietta Alboni in opera. She had, as a matter of fact, left the stage when I was precisely two years old. But I heard her sing twice: once at the Albert Hall in Rossini's " Messe Solennelle " in 1871 ; and at a private concert given by my friend, Alessandro Romili, the accompanist.[1] She was then in her 49th year, and virtually in full possession of her marvellous powers. Her husband, the Conte di Pepoli, had insisted upon her withdrawing from operatic life so long before as 1858, and the voice I heard in the Welbeck Street drawing-room sounded to my ears as fresh, rich, and powerful as that of a woman half her age.

Alboni had made her début at La Scala in 1843,

[1] This concert has been mentioned in my *Thirty Years of Musical Life*. It was doubly notable for me ; first, because Alboni sang, and, secondly, because my brother Max (then a boy of thirteen) played a violin solo. Unfortunately a string broke just as he was about to begin, and he was so upset that he burst into tears ; whereupon the famous singer, who was sitting among the listeners, went to my brother and kissed and comforted him before the whole audience. It did not take him long then to mend his string and start his piece.

when she was just twenty. Very wonderful, according to all accounts, was the organ-like contralto voice of the girl from the Romagna who went to Bologna to study under Mme Bertolatti.[1] Wonderful, too, must it have been to hear her sing Arsace to Grisi's Semiramide on the April night in 1847 when she made her London début, and which, by the way, was also the night when the doors of the newly-built Royal Italian Opera-house, Covent Garden, were opened for the first time.

For until then she had remained the true Alboni, with the " rich, deep real *contralto* of two octaves from G to G—as sweet as honey "—described by Chorley, and unimpaired or modified in quality by her subsequent stretching of its compass in the soprano direction. Previous to that experiment, the *difficile* English critic could "recollect no low Italian voice so luscious ". Afterwards, he said, although "the required high notes were forthcoming, the entire texture of the voice was injured ; its luscious quality, and some of its power, were inevitably lost ".

But not, as I have good reason to believe, permanently. There may have been a difference perceptible to the sensitive ears of Chorley. In the general opinion, however, Alboni's never ceased to be a magnificent organ, even during the period when she was singing relatively high parts such as Ninetta (*Gazza Ladra*), Zerlina, Amina, and Rosina. And that period, after all, was not an exceedingly long one. Indeed, Alboni's entire stage career extended to no more than fifteen years, during which she was

---

[1] Whilst there, half trained, she had also worked with Rossini himself at his own operas, whereof, Fétis says, he " imparted to her the pure traditions ".

assuredly singing more contralto than soprano rôles in those old Italian operas that we never hear nowadays.

When she abandoned the stage she also gave up singing music that did not lie easily in the contralto range. Hence the strain, if there was any, can hardly have been of sufficient duration to produce lasting bad effects. Anyhow, such as may have been perceived in the fifties were deemed by good judges like Manuel Garcia to have practically disappeared by the time she came to London again among the Paris exiles during the siege of 1870-71. Not long after that, my old master said to me, " She is as incomparable as ever ".

The smiling, gracious, but very stout lady to whom I was presented certainly did look like the kind of artistic personality described by Chorley in the chapter on " Mademoiselle Alboni " in the second volume of his *Recollections*.[1] It was his conviction (and he was not alone in it) that her physical development—" There was never such a personation of teeming and genial prosperity seen in Woman's form "—was largely responsible for the " absence of vivacity, of variety of dramatic instinct, which has made Mme Alboni's many delicious qualities pall after a time. Her singing has always been too monochromatic ". The writer went even further : her style, according to him, was monotonous : " Once having heard any song by Madame Alboni, and it was to be heard, for ever afterwards, unchanged and the same ".

[1] Now published in a single volume, edited by Ernest Newman.

2

That was the solitary loophole that hypercriticism could discover in her singing or, for that matter, her acting. There was not, it was said, enough life or energy or colour in what she did. Well, how could it be otherwise in one whose "face, with its broad, sunny Italian beauty, incapable of frown, and her figure were given out by Nature in some happy mood of mortal defiance to Tragedy and all its works; the features so regularly beautiful—the face so obstinately cheery, without variety; yet without vulgarity"? This lack of dramatic feeling was also noticed by the French critics when she first sang in Paris, and is referred to by Fétis, who heard her both in Paris and Brussels at various periods of her career. He adds that when "she dared to undertake a rôle like that of Fidès in *Le Prophète* at the Paris Opéra the most brilliant success rewarded her temerity"; while "an improvement previously noticed in her acting became still more pronounced in Meyerbeer's work—not that there was more passion in the accents of her voice, but increased animation in her stage gestures".

It was, in very truth, the genuinely "glorious contralto" described by Chorley that I heard in 1871. I confess I have only a vague recollection of what Alboni's voice sounded like in the Albert Hall. But, in the house nearly opposite our own at the corner of Bentinck Street and Welbeck Street, it fell upon my youthful ears with a "charm of quality and organ-like richness of volume" that I have never forgotten; different, moreover, in its deep, mellow, sonorous timbre and its close resemblance to a man's velvety tenor, from any other contralto I have ever listened to.

Three years before, she had sung with Adelina Patti the duet "Quis est homo", from Rossini's *Stabat Mater*, at the funeral in Paris of the master to whom both owed a lasting debt of gratitude. In 1894, when Alboni died in her 71st year, I happened to be staying at Craig-y-Nos Castle soon after the news arrived, and I asked Mme Patti whether she remembered singing the duet at Rossini's funeral. "Can I ever forget it?" was her reply. "Poor dear Alboni and I were so near to tears all the time we were singing that we could scarcely get through the cadenza; and, when we had finished, we both sat down and burst out weeping at the same instant"!

Alessandro Romili knew Alboni well. He had acted for some time as accompanist to Delle Sedie, a popular baritone singer and teacher, and she had frequently visited the latter's studio in Paris. Hence her singing for Romili in London. "She has the kindest disposition", he said, " of any artist I know. I have heard that she was never known to lose her temper, and you have only to look at that happy expression on her face—*car c'est toujours là*—to believe that it is true. She is the soul of generosity; her French friends simply adore her. She often sings for charity, and, whenever she does, all the contraltos in Paris go to take a lesson from her". He added that she had preserved her voice even better than Pauline Viardot-Garcia, who was sometimes called a contralto, but had never been other than a pure mezzo-soprano.

After the death of the Conte di Pepoli she married again. Nevertheless, she celebrated in 1892 the fiftieth anniversary of her *first* marriage, and gave a grand party to her friends in Paris in honour of what the invitation described as her "golden wedding". The entertainment included a concert in which the hostess took part, singing with marvellous charm the air, "Ah, se tu m'ami", from Vaccaj's *Romeo e Giulietta*. According to Mme Mathilde Marchesi, "Her house was a musical centre, and she used to give brilliant receptions. . . . She was afflicted with a stoutness which gave her great difficulty in walking, but her voice was round and full to the very last. She left a considerable fortune, part of which was bequeathed to the Paris poor".

M

II. JANET MONACH PATEY

I

Madame Patey, as she was always called, succeeded
Mme Sainton-Dolby on her retirement in 1870 as the
leading English contralto of her time. That position
she held by universal acknowledgment until her
death on February 28th, 1894, when three months short
of her 52nd birthday. Patey's place has never been
filled. Other British contraltos have earned popularity, but scarcely one has exemplified the art of
oratorio singing at the exalted level that she maintained. It has distinctly deteriorated since then,
chiefly because the demand for oratorio has diminished
to such an extent that singers with big names no longer
seek in it either the profit or the glory that it yielded
so plentifully in the past.

Patey first made her name at the Three Choirs'
(Worcester) Festival of 1866, just as her gifted tenor
colleague, Edward Lloyd, made his at the Gloucester
Festival five years later. Thenceforward oratorio held
them under its sway for good. I heard them both at
the Handel Festival of 1874, when their singing had
attained the sublimity—nothing less—of absolute
perfection. Anything more superb than Patey's
" Return, O God of Hosts " or Lloyd's " Love in her
eyes " it would have been utterly impossible to
imagine. A decade later these two had earned, in
conjunction with Albani and Santley, the joint title

of the " Representative English Quartet "—bestowed as a kind of distinction to indicate the growing emancipation of oratorio from the yoke or, rather, the monopoly of the foreign artist.

A Londoner by birth and a Scotswoman by parentage, Janet Patey was blessed with comparatively few advantages in the way of musical training. Some early vocal instruction from John Wass ; a little " coaching " from the wife of Sims Reeves and from Pinsuti, the song-composer ; two or three years in Henry Leslie's Choir—the last a valuable experience for acquiring musicianship and artistic taste—comprised the whole story. I remember once hearing something about a brief visit to Italy and a few months under the famous teacher, Sangiovanni ; but for the truth of that I cannot vouch.

Personally she was not prepossessing. Many a time I used to reflect how odd it was that the hard, almost masculine, face should conceal a capacity for such womanly tenderness, such serene beauty of religious expression. But the absence of facial charm was more than atoned for by the ravishing quality of her voice and the nobility of her style. Her singing could breathe the very soul of consolation, faith and hope.[1]

Her fame was by no means confined to her native country. Her enterprising husband, John G. Patey (a well-known baritone singer), arranged a concert

[1] Writing in the *Sunday Times* a few days after her death, I said :

" In its prime Madame Patey's voice was remarkable for its evenness no less than its surpassing beauty of quality. The medium was deliciously mellow, and the richness and power of the chest notes throughout nearly a whole octave used to thrill an audience as deeply as the ringing head tones of a Clara tour for her in America in 1871, with Edith Wynne (soprano), W. H. Cummings (tenor), Santley and himself for her associates. That trip first earned her international fame. In 1875 she made an appearance in Paris at the concerts conducted by Lamoureux at the Cirque des Champs-Elysées. There her singing in a French performance of the *Messiah* contributed largely to an extraordinary success that resulted in no fewer than three repetitions of Handel's masterpiece. Subsequently, when she sang at the Conservatoire, the directors paid her the unwonted compliment of having a gold medal of honour specially struck for her, bearing the dates of the concerts.

2

I heard her first in *Elijah* at the Norwich Festival of 1875. By then her services were in request at all the principal festivals, Trebelli being practically the only other singer to whom leading contralto parts were entrusted. But, great as was my admiration for the popular Frenchwoman, I am fain to admit that in the *Messiah* and *Elijah* she was not the equal of Patey, in whom spontaneity and impulse were replaced by other gifts perhaps even more vital, more essential to the ideal interpretation of sacred music. There was a certain dignity and impressiveness, a calm assurance of religious sincerity, reflected alike in her manner and Novello or a Lemmens-Sherrington. . . . Her delivery of such airs as ' He was depised ' and ' O rest in the Lord ' was a triumph of fervid yet unaffected religious expression and purity of vocal style. Such operatic airs as suited her, she sang well, but after oratorio she was at her best in a simple ballad, which she understood the secret of adorning with just so much art as it would stand and no more ".

delivery, that seemed to match the simple grandeur of her swelling notes and her eloquent outpouring of unimpassioned feeling. When she rose slowly, score in hand, to sing " He was despised " or " O rest in the Lord " you prepared for the thrill that was to come ; and it never failed. The voice, the words, the music, all seemed to be utterly detached from merely human, terrestrial surroundings. Even when heard in the interior of one of our glorious old Gothic cathedrals, the piece resolved itself into a purely spiritual message.

Yet there was reason for doubting whether this quiet, unagitated exterior, so characteristic of the resolute woman, afforded a true indication of the nervous turmoil that was stirring beneath the surface. It was not emotional in the ordinary sense. Often enough Patey gave plain evidence of dramatic power, as for instance in the spiteful utterances of Queen Jezebel in the second part of *Elijah* ; but I cannot remember at any time the least outward indication of her being directly moved by a strong temperamental influence. I was told, however, that she frequently sang, after passing the middle of her career, under considerable mental strain, and that it tended to increase as the years went on.

Early in the nineties she undertook a lengthy tour in Australia, and was constantly travelling for nearly a couple of years at a period when facilities for covering big distances were not as convenient as they are to-day. She returned so fatigued that we noticed the change on her reappearance at a Crystal Palace concert in October, 1891. The further diminution of her breathing capacity and vocal power was very palpable on the last occasion that I heard her—namely, at a Patti concert at the Albert Hall on July 1st, 1893.

The fact is that neither she herself nor those around her seemed to realize how ill she was. The end, when it came suddenly within a few hours of her singing at Sheffield, on February 28th, 1894, reminded one of the tragic ending to the lives of Malibran and Tietjens. Mme Patey had sung at Newark the night before; and the Sheffield audience insisted upon an encore after her rendering of Handel's " Lascia ch'io pianga ". She gave them " The Banks of Allan Water ", and had scarcely uttered the concluding line—" And there a corpse lay she "—when she fainted, and had to be carried from the concert-room to her hotel. Nor did she regain consciousness before her death, which occurred early on the following morning. The great English contralto had died literally " in harness ".

A

III. SOFIA SCALCHI

The late James Henry Mapleson declared in his *Memoirs* that he " discovered Mdlle Scalchi, the eminent contralto ", during his autumn season at Covent Garden in 1868. As a matter of fact, he had not far to look in order to accomplish that feat or to secure his *trouvaille*. In the previous September she was singing at some Promenade Concerts held at the Agricultural Hall, Islington, which the impresario, with his customary bluntness, described as " a building which had been a circus ". If there was any discovery at all, the credit for it was due to the musical critics, who were almost unanimously of opinion that " Mdlle " Scalchi was the possessor of a phenomenal organ and deserving of trial in a *milieu* worthier of her gifts.

Her success was consequently a foregone conclusion when she made her first stage appearance in this country as Azucena in *Il Trovatore* on the 5th of the following November. It amounted, indeed, to a triumph, and ensured her re-engagement for the " coalition season " of the summer of 1869. Thenceforward she sang at Covent Garden for twenty consecutive years—*i.e.*, throughout the remainder of the Gye régime and during two seasons under Augustus Harris.

At the time of her London début Sofia Scalchi was a robust, buxom, broad-chested girl of only eighteen ;

yet by no means without stage experience. (Born at Turin on November 29th, 1850, she had come out at Mantua in 1866 as Ulrica in *Un Ballo in Maschera*.) With Trebelli in his company, Mapleson had no pressing need of another leading contralto. Consequently Scalchi signed a long contract with the rival impresario, and by 1872 had made herself a recognized favourite, as Mr Gye declared, " not only by the charm of her beautiful voice, but by her unvarying conscientious and careful performances ". She made her mark then more especially in Cimarosa's delightful opera, *Le Astuzie Femminili ;* later on as Edwige in *Guillaume Tell ;* and in parts such as Urbano in *Les Huguenots,* Maffio Orsini in *Lucrezia Borgia,* Siebel in *Faust,* the Caprajo in *Dinorah,* Pierotto in *Linda di Chamouni,* as Leonora in *La Favorita,* and Azucena in *Il Trovatore.*

I heard her in course of time in all but the first of the parts just named. Subsequently came the notable impersonations of her riper period, *viz.,* Amneris in *Aïda,* Fidès in *Le Prophète,* and Arsace in *Semiramide.* By degrees, therefore, her repertory became a fairly extensive one ; and, as her popularity augmented here, so did the Italian contralto have to respond to increasing demands for her services elsewhere. She never sang, however, in any language save her own.

Scalchi's was a gorgeous voice—one of those genuine Italian contraltos of the Alboni type, with an organ's breadth of tone and a resonant ring that could fill with ease the largest auditorium. The chest notes were powerful down to F ; the head register smooth, round, and clear right up to the B flat or even high C. It had, moreover, a flexible texture, with a singularly smooth, even scale and sufficient executive brilliancy for the Rossinian runs and cadenzas.

SOFIA SCALCHI

She was never a particularly good actress; just adequate and no more. Blessed by nature with an exceptionally large mouth, she generally kept it closed when she was not singing, or else allowed it when open to expand into a broad smile. This limited her shades of facial expression—wherein she compared disadvantageously with Trebelli, who, though not a genuine contralto, sang exactly the same line of parts. Thus one critic, writing in April 1880, about a revival of *Les Huguenots*, said : " Next to Mme Trebelli, Mlle. Scalchi is the best Urbano of modern times ". Another opined that " Mme Trebelli's Urbano remains what it always has been—the best presented since the time of Alboni ".

Attractive as her assumption of Meyerbeer's Page undoubtedly was, Scalchi surpassed it both vocally and histrionically with her embodiment of Arsace. She sang this first in 1878, when Patti, who had refused to appear in *Semiramide* during Tietjens's lifetime, essayed the rôle of the Assyrian queen at Covent Garden. I have recorded in *The Reign of Patti* the " extraordinary effect " that the *diva* " created with Scalchi in the famous duet, ' Giorno d'orrore ' ". This triumph they always repeated so long as they continued to appear together in Rossini's opera.[1]

It should be noted that Scalchi was the Leonora in

[1] In 1883 the critic of *The Daily Telegraph* (Joseph Bennett) referred to the two famous singers in the following characteristic terms : " Patti can sing the music better than anyone else, and that is enough. Her triumph was a familiar one, the old points being made with the results that have never failed since she first assumed the part. Madame Scalchi divided honours with the prima donna. Arsace is her greatest rôle, and she delivers the pure Italian music as to the manner born—which indeed may be truly said of her ".

La Favorita when Mario made his farewell appearance at Covent Garden in Donizetti's opera (July 19th, 1871), and during the same season she also sang with him in *Faust*, *Les Huguenots*, and *Il Matrimonio Segreto*. The great tenor had a marked admiration for her magnificent voice; and all who ever heard her would have agreed that he was right. The pity is that as time goes on contraltos of the Alboni-Scalchi type tend more and more to disappear from our ken. Their unique combination of voice and art has already done so.

IV. GIULIA RAVOGLI

I

In the autumn of 1890 a season of Italian opera was given at Covent Garden by one Antonio Lago, a venturesome but capable impresario, who had earned experience at that house in the service of Frederic Gye, and was now striving to follow in his footsteps.

Unluckily for his chance, he found himself "up against" the superior genius of Sir Augustus Harris. Yet, during his brief campaign Lago contrived to introduce several unknown artists of exceptional merit, among them two sisters of Italian birth, named Sofia and Giulia Ravogli, of whom the latter was destined to make her mark among the surviving great contraltos of the operatic stage. The sisters, who had come from their native land with a high reputation, made their débuts here on October 18th in *Aïda*, filling the rôles of the heroine and Amneris in such fashion as to create a highly favourable impression.

It was not, however, until three weeks later that a revival of Gluck's *Orfeo* (after an interval of thirty years at Covent Garden) revealed the full beauty and range of Giulia Ravogli's vocal and histrionic gifts. Not easily can one forget the delight of hearing Gluck's *chef-d'œuvre* worthily performed for the first time, especially when enhanced by the noble impersonation and finished singing of an Orfeo whom the older critics thought worthy of comparison with her illustrious predecessor in the part, Pauline Viardot-Garcia. This achievement lifted the newcomer forthwith to the top of the tree. Each time the opera was given big audiences crowded the theatre to acclaim Giulia Ravogli, together with her sister Sofia who, if her talents stood upon a lower plane, nevertheless imparted conspicuous charm and poetic quality to the character of Eurydice.[1]

Soon everyone was asking, "Who are these Ravogli sisters? Why have we never heard them before?" The fact was that Signor Lago and his popular conductor, Enrico Bevignani, had only come across them at the Teatro Manzoni in Milan in the previous spring. He had then discovered also that if he wanted to engage one sister he would be obliged to take the other. They had pursued a joint career from the start. Still, this stipulation was no great hardship; for if Giulia was the more richly endowed of the two, Sofia was likewise an accomplished artist, being unusually beautiful to look upon (both sisters were "divinely tall") and capable of using her fine soprano voice with conspicuous skill. When in after years Sofia died, Giulia also said farewell to the

[1] In the *Sunday Times* of November 9, 1890, I wrote as follows :

" Mlle Ravogli impressed by her eloquent gestures over the tomb of Eurydice and the pathetic accents of her mourning in the air ' Chiamo il mio ben cosî '; but the first real effect worth mentioning was her delivery of the interpolated air by Bertoni, and this superb piece of vocalization, terminating with the extraordinarily difficult cadenza which Mme Viardot wrote and sang herself, created a positive sensation. The vigour and breadth of the declamation, the brilliancy, the precision and the beauty of voice with which the *fiorituri* were sung, and, lastly, the execution of a long descending chromatic scale, even and true as a string of pearls, fairly took the house by storm ".

GIULIA RAVOGLI AS ORFEO

theatre and, being then happily married to the late well-known surgeon, Mr Harrison Cripps (brother of the present Lord Parmoor), went into the peaceful retirement which, as these lines are written, she still enjoys.

Giulia Ravogli was born at Rome on March 3rd, 1860. She attended until she was thirteen a Catholic college; and it was there that the exceptional beauty of her voice first aroused attention. At home—as in the case of Adelina Patti—her people would place her on a table and let her warble *canti popolari* and operatic melodies to her heart's content. But at the college, when her voice gradually matured and displayed an abnormally full, masculine timbre, they used to call her " Il Tenore " and made good use of her in their choir. The consequence was that at the age of 15 she was taken with Sofia to Milan to study with Signora Abbadia. Four years' steady training made capable artists of them both. In 1879 the sisters won an immediate success on their débuts at Malta in Bellini's *Norma ;* Sofia singing the title-rôle and Giulia that of Adalgisa.

Then came a spell of constant touring in Italy for several years in this and other operas. It was whilst they were appearing in *Semiramide* at Milan in 1889 that the courteous head of the house of Ricordi— the Cavaliere Giulio Ricordi—sent for them and suggested their taking part in a revival of Gluck's *Orfeo,* an opera then sadly neglected everywhere. He was particularly anxious to see *Orfeo* well mounted and sung in the Lombardian capital; and it struck him that the Ravoglis were just the artists to realize the ideal Orpheus and Eurydice.

The event proved Signor Ricordi to have been not

far wrong. First, as they had never seen the opera, they went to Venice to witness a performance of it there with the German mezzo-soprano, Hélène Hastreiter, whom Mapleson in 1887 had introduced to London in *La Favorita*. Vocally speaking, however, Giulia was to prove much more acceptable to English audiences than Fräulein Hastreiter, who, in my opinion, " was not particularly sympathetic, nor was her intonation of high notes reliable ". Eventually in 1889 *Orfeo* was produced at the Teatro Manzoni, Milan, and it carried the name and fame of the Roman singer to the farthest corners of Italy. At about the same period the sisters were singing with success in the principal opera-houses at Berlin, Munich, Vienna, and Barcelona.

2

It was not in *Orfeo*, as has been said, that the Ravoglis made their London début; but during the interval between their *Aïda* performance and the Gluck revival they appeared in other operas. Giulia, I remember, created an especially vivid impression by her dashing embodiment of Urbano in *Les Huguenots*, which was the more creditable because it was so completely different in *genre* from the calm, classical dignity of her Orfeo.

In the meantime, too, the famous pre-Raphaelite painter, Sir Edward Burne-Jones, R.A., had become interested in the Italian contralto and insisted on designing a new Orpheus costume for her. This was accordingly made in London, with draperies in the purest Greek style, the original drawing for which still remains among the singer's treasured possessions. When the curtain went up on the night of her first appearance and she stood mourning, lyre in hand, over the grave of the dead Eurydice, Giulia Ravogli in the exquisite Burne-Jones dress made a superb and impressive picture. Her glorious singing did the rest.

The voice was not, strictly speaking, a deep contralto, but rather a mezzo-contralto with an unusual range in the upper register. Nevertheless the low notes down to G and F had abundant richness and power; while the quality of the medium conveyed a measure of pathos so profound that at certain moments it was sure to " bring a lump " to one's throat. Hence the extraordinarily touching effect of her " Che farò ". The tone, the accent, the phrasing, all combined with every inflection and every gesture to depict with overwhelming force what Orpheus felt when bereft for the second time of his beloved Eurydice. The immense breath-control and complete mastery of the *messa di voce* were similarly striking. In short, here was an artist in the direct line of the great singers.

3

Until 1896 Giulia Ravogli remained a regular member of what was at that time the finest international operatic organization in the world. Her repertory grew steadily larger and exceptionally varied. In the revival of Ponchielli's *La Gioconda* in 1890 she did not sing the contralto part of La Cieca but the mezzo-soprano one of Laura. Next season in *Martha* she was the Nancy; while in *Lohengrin* her intensely dramatic Ortrud took even her friends by surprise.

Her Carmen, though much admired, suffered by immediate comparison with Calvé's; in 1895 she sang Fidès to the Jean de Leyden of Tamagno in a notable revival of *Le Prophète;* while her Mignon, Zerlina, and Mistress Quickly (*Falstaff*) testified further to her versatility. One of her last appearances at Covent Garden was in 1899, when she sang Adalgisa (her earliest rôle) to the Norma of Lilli Lehmann and the Oroveso of Plançon.

Giulia Ravogli's successful career in oratorio formed a conspicuous feature of her English artistic life. Sir Charles Santley was her instructor, and she quickly obtained recognition as one of the best oratorio vocalists of the day. Engaged for all the important provincial Festivals, the Royal Albert Hall, etc., she distinguished herself by her consistently admirable work in all the popular masterpieces. During her all-too-brief career she captured universal regard and esteem, alike by the abundance of her gifts and the charm of her smiling, sunny disposition.

V. ERNESTINE SCHUMANN-HEINK

It was plain "Frau Heink" when the name first appeared upon a Covent Garden programme in 1892. Until then London had not even heard it, and barely noticed it now among the company sent over by Pollini, of Hamburg, to sing German opera here under an unknown young conductor—Gustav Mahler. It was wonderful how anybody got noticed at all. Seventy-five artists in ten weeks is something of a crowd; and who was to know that the majority of them, not actual celebrities then, were to become so in course of that productive decade?

Ernestine Heink was already the mother of four children, but not yet wedded to her second husband, Paul Schumann, an actor. She was Bohemian by birth; a native of the little town of Lieben, near Prague (July 15th, 1861). She had been trained at Graz and Dresden; had sung at Graz as contralto soloist in Beethoven's Choral Symphony when she was fifteen; and had won acceptance at Dresden and Hamburg for several years after her original "hit" at Kroll's Theatre, Berlin, in 1881.

Already full of experience, she was engaged now for the first performances of the *Ring* that had been given in London since Angelo Neumann's production at Her Majesty's ten years before; and Mahler was to make of the revival an historic event. Amid this matchless throng it was not easy for any individual to excel.

Yet there appeared a quality in Frau Heink's voice, an artistry in her singing and acting and her work generally, that was too exceptional to escape remark. Erda in *Siegfried* was not a very helpful part, either, to make a début in. It was the first year that the Cimmerian darkness of Bayreuth had been ventured upon in the fashionable *milieu* of Covent Garden; and the imitation was so thoroughly carried out that the thin shaft of silvery light reflected upon Erda was barely powerful enough to make her head visible.

Her voice, however, emerged distinctly enough, and what we heard was so entrancing in its solemn, mystical beauty, its breadth, firmness and volume, that we would fain have listened to Erda a good deal more. For the full revelation of her unique tone, together with the singer's extraordinary gift of pathetic and touching expression, we had to wait for her Waltraute in *Götterdämmerung*.[1] Frau Cosima Wagner thought her Waltraute the finest that had ever been heard, and raved over her equally perfect Brangäne in *Tristan und Isolde*. Bayreuth was to acknowledge the greatness of both those impersonations.

She was a past-mistress in comic as well as tragic parts. When Harris brought out Nessler's *Der Trompeter von Säkkingen* she evoked the loudest laughter of the evening as the watchful old Gräfin, whilst singing her music with infinite spirit and a true sense of character. Again, a few nights later, she afforded an example of genuine *esprit d'ensemble* by undertaking the insignificant part of the Shepherd in

---

[1] It was, by the way, Mahler who now restored her intensely moving scene with Brünnhilde, which had unaccountably been omitted by Seidl at Her Majesty's.

ERNESTINE SCHUMANN-HEINK

Tannhäuser, among a memorable group that included Klafsky, Bettaque, Alvary, Reichmann, and Wiegand.[1]

Re-engaged for London in 1898, she made a deeper impression than before. Her powers had ripened. Her voice had gained measurably in plenitude of volume and gloriously rich tone; her acting had grown in dignity and assurance as well as, when required, wealth of humour. Her Erda was again unsurpassable. In the opening section of the *Ring* she would double with that character the third Rhine-daughter; in *Die Walküre* her magnificent Fricka would be followed up by her Waltraute (among the Valkyries); and, again in *Götterdämmerung* by the Flosshilde of the Rhine scene. In short, she proved herself, as was remarked at the time, " a great artist, to whom no task ever came amiss ".[2]

But Schumann-Heink's chief successes of '98 were Brangäne and Magdalena, particularly the latter. Jean de Reszke—" the ideal Walther of our dreams "—sang his rôle in German for the first time; Scheidemantel was the Hans Sachs (perhaps another " best ever "); David Bispham made an admirable Beckmesser; and Johanna Gadski the finest Eva we had had in London with the single exception of Rosa Sucher. Finally, " The Magdalena was worthy of her mistress. In her hands it was simply a delightful

---

[1] That night Gustav Mahler conducted in London for the last time. He came an unknown man, and quitted these shores to build up, ere he died, a lasting reputation in Vienna and New York.

[2] The German conductor that year was Felix Mottl; the Siegfried and Hagen were Jean and Edouard de Reszke; the Brünnhildes Lillian Nordica and Milka Ternina; the Wotan Anton van Rooy; the Loge Ernest van Dyck. Finer casts have never been heard here.

creation, lacking in nothing that could lend it consistency and interest ".

In the same week she appeared before Queen Victoria at Windsor Castle in an abbreviated version of *Lohengrin,* her companions being Jean and Edouard de Reszke, Bispham, and Lillian Nordica. The Queen had never previously heard either *Lohengrin* nor the famous Polish brothers. In connection with the presentation of the customary Royal souvenirs after the performance an amusing episode occurred, which I thus related at the time :

"It is usual on these occasions for the leading artists hurriedly to throw off their costumes, don evening dress, and await the command to be introduced into the Queen's presence. Now MM. Jean and Edouard de Reszke had never appeared before her Majesty in opera before, and, like the practical men that they are, had determined to avoid the inconvenience of dressing at Windsor. They accordingly left London in the evening fully attired as Lohengrin and Henrich der Vogler, but covered with dark cloaks so as to avoid the inquisitive gaze of a Cockney crowd. The plan no doubt saved them much hurry and trouble ; but the consequence was that, when the moment came for the presentation, the gifted brothers had only their operatic costumes wherein to appear before the Queen of England. Imagine the consternation of the Court officials! One, it is said, proposed to run and fetch a ' Windsor uniform ' and see if it would fit M. Jean ; another smilingly suggested that M. Edouard would look well in the Elizabethan garments of a beefeater, whereof a large stock in various sizes is always kept on hand at the Castle.

" In the end the two singers were presented to her Majesty in their own handsome costumes of the Lohengrin period. The strange contrast no doubt created something of a sensation, particularly as the Telramund of the evening,

Mr. David Bispham, had put on faultless evening dress, and even Mme. Nordica and Frau Schumann-Heink had contrived to exchange their stage gowns for becoming modern *peignoirs*. However, it made no difference whatever to the Queen, who graciously conversed for some time with both the brothers, expressing the delight it had afforded her to hear them in opera at last and to listen to ' the beautiful music' of Wagner's work; while M. Jean de Reszke for his part spoke of the deep and infinite pleasure that they had experienced in thus contributing to the Queen's pleasure upon her Majesty's 80th birthday ''.

During the same season Frau Schumann-Heink took advantage of being in London to make a brief adventure in the direction of oratorio, as sung in the English language, for which purpose I gave her a few lessons in pronunciation and diction. Many will remember more especially her rendering " But the Lord is mindful of His own ", from Mendelssohn's *St. Paul*. I never heard her sing it in public, but in America it was constantly in demand for her recital programmes. She did not, however, seriously follow up the oratorio idea.

In the United States I came across Mme Schumann-Heink again early in 1902. She had gone there under the management of Maurice Grau, and made her début at the Chicago Auditorium. Subsequently, she became for a time a favourite at the Metropolitan Opera House, New York. Still greater, though, was her success as a concert artist, and she made a fortune by the recitals she gave on her own account in every State of the Union.

It was the same in Lieder-singing as in opera—everything came alike to this rarely-gifted vocalist. Hence, partly, her inability to say " no " when in

1904 a seductive theatre manager came along with a dazzling offer for her to tour the States with a comic opera, called *Love's Lottery*, by the English composer, Julian Edwards.   The part of the heroine had been cleverly devised to fit a mature contralto of 45, and for her at least the venture proved a huge success.   It was said that in less than two years she netted nearly a quarter of a million dollars.

In 1909 she came to Europe and created the part of Klytemnestra in Richard Strauss's *Elektra* at Dresden. Five years later she obtained a divorce from her third husband, and she still dwells, like a good American citizen, in the country of her choice to enjoy the fruits of her long life of hard work.   In October, 1926, she undertook a farewell tour and gave what was supposed to be her final recital in the city of New York.

VI. ANTOINETTE STERLING

There are doubtless many besides the present writer who remember this singer's beautiful voice— its true contralto timbre, the purity and richness of it, and its capacity for deep, earnest expression. To my ears it always had a familiar ring, because Manuel Garcia was teaching at our house in Bentinck Street when she came to him for lessons in the mid-seventies. I was myself studying with the grand old maestro at the time, and used to hear her going over the difficult old Italian airs with which he was so fond of training his advanced pupils. She had not long married, and her husband, John Mackinlay, was as ambitious for her as her teacher; but the benefit derived from the old-fashioned *fiorituri* was quite indirect, for she never sang them in public. Antoinette Sterling, however eclectic in her taste and her artistry, was known to the world that loved and admired her purely as an oratorio and a ballad singer.

She was by birth American, but of British descent; and the blend of the two nationalities accounted in a way for her peculiar strength and individuality of character. In her work, as in her daily trend of thought, she was above all things original and refined. A stickler for traditional style, she would nevertheless impart to the most hackneyed oratorio airs a rendering, alike in phrasing and touches of expressive feeling, that always seemed to be essentially her own. Certainly she never copied anyone. For this reason, apart from the sheer loveliness of her organ (so long as it remained fresh and " unforced ") she was invariably an interesting artist to listen to. For example, her reading of the *Messiah* and *Elijah* solos sounded quite different from Mme Patey's, yet it was no less imbued with earnest piety, religious reverence, and devotional sentiment.

Antoinette Sterling possessed in a singular degree the art of suiting her theme to her audience, and this with a repertory at command that was by no means unusually extensive. Her public at the Ballad Concerts, where she sang for many years, loved her for the strong dramatic sense that coloured her songs, old or new, and she never failed, as I well remember, to extract the last grain of effect from things like " The Lost Chord ", " The Sands of Dee ", and " The Three Fishers ". On the other hand she also knew exactly how to interpret the Lieder of Schubert and Schumann to the satisfaction of the more critical amateurs who frequented the " Pops ". Her only fault there was a tendency to allow her chest-register too much play in passages where a softer medium tone would have answered the purpose better. But at any rate she never failed to obey Garcia's behest not to carry her voice either too high or too low, but limit it to its exceptionally full contralto range from low F to high C. Her earlier teachers, Mmes Viardot and Marchesi, had not been so particular.

She died at Hampstead in 1904, after a long and highly successful career, in course of which she took part in all the leading musical festivals and choral and other important concerts both in and out of the metropolis. In a word, she was one of the great contraltos of her epoch, and I may add that, despite her outspoken candour on most subjects, she was an exceptional favourite with her fellow-artists.

▲

THE GREAT WAGNERIAN SOPRANOS

It is probable that the future musical historian will fix upon the Albert Hall Festival of 1877 as the event that started the true crystallization of Wagnerian opinion in this country. One thing is certain. If it did so in regard to the music of the Bayreuth master, it did so no less effectually in regard to the *nouveau art* of the singers who came here to interpret it. Their share in the display was tantamount to a revelation. It opened up an entirely fresh line of vocal treatment, a new technique of declamatory art; and it introduced to British audiences a type of German opera singer previously unknown here.

During his stay in London Wagner made allusion more than once to the devotion of the distinguished artists who a year previously had taken part in the first complete performance of *Der Ring des Nibelungen* at Bayreuth. Some of them were then following in his train at their inconvenience, perhaps loss, to help in raising the balance owing for the erection of his theatre.[1] And our public had almost as much reason to be grateful to them; for, had it not been for their

[1] I remember particularly his referring to this in a little speech he made at the supper given for him on the eve of the Festival, when I had the privilege of being presented and speaking to him.

spirit of loyalty and self-sacrifice, we in this country should most likely never have heard any of those celebrated men and women who were in the original cast of the *Ring*.

Well-trained, experienced artists, they afforded living justification for Wagner's *dictum* that only singers reared in the old Italian school were capable of interpreting his music in the manner that he had intended—that was, of combining his system of declamation with the art of the *bel canto*. Heretofore most of his vocal writing had been looked upon as a kind of glorified rhythmical recitative, sometimes very dull to listen to and nearly always harmful to the singer. Vocal selections from the *Ring, Tristan,* and *Die Meistersinger* had not been heard here at all until they were given at this Festival, and the manner of their rendering put an entirely different complexion upon a very vexed problem.

Music which we had regarded as unsingable flowed from the lips of these accredited interpreters with a freedom and ease wholly undreamt of " in our philosophy ". They did not invariably give us the impeccable *legato*, the exquisite smoothness of the Italian *cantilena*; not perhaps because they were unable to, but because the music would not have sounded right had they done so. They brought instead a new kind of plastic beauty, together with a greater depth and energy of expression; a more profound dramatic significance accompanying a strong consonantal utterance of every syllable in Wagner's alliterative text. This was an altogether novel combination. It enabled us to perceive the possible existence in this strange music of a hidden melodic charm of irresistible potency, apart from that unfolding of gorgeous orchestral sonority and colour which excerpts from the later scores of the master had already partially revealed. This better understanding was the first real step in the process leading to a change in our national attitude towards what was then still styled the " Music of the Future ".

The second stage did not begin until five years later. We may consider as negligible—valuable though they were at the time—the Italian and English performances of *Lohengrin*, *Tannhäuser*, *The Flying Dutchman*, and even *Rienzi*, given during the interval between 1877 and 1882. They were no more than the *hors-d'œuvres* which whetted our appetite for the heavier dishes. But it was an appetite that was growing at a tremendous rate when our year of realization arrived. An absolute clash of the two big German undertakings—Angelo Neumann's cycles of *Der Ring* at Her Majesty's with the Pollini-Franke season at Drury Lane—was only avoided by a hair's-breadth. Happily they were neither of them in excess of our half-developed capacity for the enjoyment and appreciation of Wagner in his noblest manifestations.

The troupes that came over in 1882 were recruited from the opera-houses at Hamburg, Leipzig, Berlin, Dresden, and Munich. They were, of course, wholly separate organizations, Anton Seidl conducting the tetralogy and Hans Richter the other series of operas. The first production of *Parsifal* at Bayreuth was imminent. The early rehearsals were even then in active progress ; but they interfered only slightly with the protagonists of the London campaign, nearly all of whom were able to complete their engagements here. With the exception of Materna, they included practically the whole of the famous sopranos whom Wagner had secured for Bayreuth that summer.

The above and two or three more comprise the illustrious group whose lives are briefly sketched in the following pages. These women were, in sooth, very great singers as well as great artists. I am not to blame if I have been unable to find in them much to criticize. The simple truth is that, taken for all in all, their art was beyond criticism, like their intelligence, their persevering industry, their intense devotion to the cause that they loved and lived for.

I. AMALIA MATERNA

Materna was not only the first and greatest of all Brünnhildes, but also the original Kundry; and she was the soprano chosen to interpret Wagner's music at the Albert Hall Festival of 1877. The master himself appointed her to each of these tasks. He apparently had her superb voice in mind when writing the tremendous parts just named; anyhow, her memory will always be associated with them. The critics who went to Bayreuth in 1876 for the production of the *Ring* returned deeply impressed with the grandeur of her performance; and, when she came to London in the following year, I was enabled to form a good idea of the sublime heights that her chief creation had attained.

I saw her at Bayreuth in 1888 as Kundry, six years after the first representation of *Parsifal*, five after Wagner's death, and fifteen before the Bayreuth right of sole possession had been rudely and successfully challenged by a German-American manager at the Metropolitan Opera House, New York. At the age of forty, Materna's Kundry was still an impersonation that combined with rare physical charm and fascination the extraordinary mixture of spiritual and human qualities that Wagner has put into the character. Like the consummate actress that she was, she differentiated with marvellous skill between the three women in one whom Kundry embodies. Most impressive of all, perhaps, were the eloquent facial expression and gestures of the silent servitor in the last act. Her voice, too, in the long scene with Parsifal in Klingsor's magic garden, still retained the same rich, vibrant timbre, together with not a little of the freshness and declamatory power that had enabled her so easily to fill the Albert Hall eleven years previously.[1] Hers was an ideal organ—governed by an ideal method—for the interpretation of Wagner's later heroines; and indeed to the art of Materna may be attributed nearly every " Bayreuth tradition " worth remembering in connection with those heroic characters.

Her early stage career had some curious features. She was born at the small town of St. Georgen (Styria, Austria) on July 10th, 1847. Her father, a schoolmaster, was too poor to give her a musical education; but the townsfolk (who had enjoyed listening to her solos at the parish church) raised sufficient money to send her to Graz, to study there with a Viennese singing teacher. Her progress was rapid, and she was barely 18 when the unusual beauty of her voice induced the local manager to engage her for the Thalia Theatre at Graz for *soubrette* parts in operetta and farce.

Such was the initial job undertaken by the future Brünnhilde at a salary of 40 gulden a month to begin with, rising to 100 gulden after the first year. On the strength of that she married an actor in the company, Karl Friedrich, and in 1867 both were engaged for the

[1] I have mentioned in *Thirty Years of Musical Life* how the size of our big hall intimidated Frau Materna when she first entered it for the rehearsal, and how I personally reassured her on the point. She took my advice and sang in her usual way without in the least " forcing " her voice. The result was that among other things she gave out the high C in the Valkyrie's " Ho-yo-to-hè " with magnificent and thrilling power.

Karl Theater in Vienna. Then began in right good earnest the study of serious operatic rôles. She was lucky enough to arouse the interest of the Kapellmeister of the Hoftheater, Heinrich Proch—he who wrote the famous Variations—and she became his pupil.

Proch taught her the rôle of Selika in *L'Africaine*. It was just what was required at that moment at the Hofoper, so Dingelstedt, the director, went to hear her and engaged her on the spot. However, he wanted her to appear first in Gluck's *Armide*, and she did so (in 1869) with unequivocal success, thus preparing the ground for a still greater triumph as Selika. The latter attracted the notice of many notable people, including Richard Wagner himself. Only, that busy man did not then need her services, and was content to bide his time.

2

Meanwhile the reputation of Amalia Materna at Vienna went up " by leaps and by bounds ". During her wonderful years at the Hofoper she sang many exacting parts ; and, as evidence of her versatility— being a fine actress as well as an accomplished dramatic singer—she was able to delight her exigent public in two such strongly-contrasted rôles as Leonora in *Fidelio* and Ortrud in *Lohengrin*—the same feat that both Tietjens and Lilli Lehmann performed a few years later. Wagner, after he had heard her in 1872, was so " *entzückt* " that he would have been willing to make sure of his Brünnhilde forthwith. It was thought wiser, however, to give her a preliminary trial as a Valkyrie in one of the early performances of *Die Walküre ;* and to this she agreed.

It may be thought strange that Frau Materna should not have re-visited London. One reason was that she had succumbed to the flattering requests of Theodore Thomas to go to the United States to take part in festivals and concerts at various cities over there. American dollars became more attractive to her than Austrian florins or even English pounds; and an offer from Dr Leopold Damrosch for his German season at the Metropolitan in 1885 was immediately accepted. When she made her operatic début in New York, to quote Krehbiel, " Mme. Materna was thirty-eight years old and her splendid powers were at their zenith ". The opera was *Tannhäuser*.

Her Elisabeth is said to have been a beautiful and wholly satisfying assumption; but by the end of a month she had also appeared as Valentine in *Les Huguenots*, Rachel in *La Juive*, and as Brünnhilde in *Die Walküre*, this last being, of course, the *clou* of the series. The part of Fricka was sustained by another renowned soprano, Marianne Brandt; nevertheless, as Krehbiel declared, " Mme. Materna was the inspiration of the performance. It was a suprise to those who had already learned to admire her to see how in the character of Brünnhilde she towered above herself in all other rôles. If anything can establish a sympathy between us and the mythological creatures of Wagner's dramas, that thing is the acting and singing of Materna ".

She remained on the stage for about a dozen years after the events above recorded, making her last public appearance on April 23rd, 1897. She then took up her residence in Vienna, where her death occurred on January 18th, 1918.

II. MARIANNE BRANDT

I

When for the first time, a lad of not quite sixteen, I had the lucky chance of hearing Patti at Covent Garden in 1872 as Zerlina in *Don Giovanni*, I had eyes and ears for no one else, unless perhaps for the great Faure in his famous embodiment of the Don. Hence my being sublimely unconscious of the fact that the Donna Elvira was a celebrated Austrian singer who had a few nights before made her début here as Leonora in *Fidelio*. It is of interest now because it happens that she was the distinguished heroine of this sketch.

Frederic Gye never re-engaged Marianne Brandt, whom he had originally wanted, by the way, to sing Ortrud if he produced *Lohengrin*. But it would be unfair to say on that account that her Donna Elvira (or her Fidelio either) was a failure at Covent Garden. Already in her 30th year, she was too gifted an artist to have completely failed in any part; and in Berlin they reckoned Donna Elvira among her best. Anyhow ten years were to elapse before she returned to London, and then it was not to Covent Garden, but to Drury Lane as a member of the historic company engaged to sing Wagner and other operas here in the German language.

Another puzzle connected with the Marianne Brandt of this period was the difficulty of " placing " her. Was she a soprano, as most Fidelios and Donna

Elviras are supposed to be? Was she the contralto that was her official designation at the Hofoper in Berlin? Or was she the mezzo-soprano subsequently identified with the greatest Brangänes and Kundrys of her day? Well, the truth is that she could be all three in turn. Her voice had an abnormal range of qualities as well as of compass and power. She had the low notes of a contralto, the high notes of a soprano, and the rich, full medium of a mezzo-soprano. But since, strictly speaking, a female singer can be classified under only one of these heads, I venture to say that Marianne Brandt was a mezzo-soprano and nothing else.

Her family name was Marie Bischof, and she was born at Vienna on September 12th, 1842. She studied there at the Conservatoire, and in 1867 came out at Graz as Rachel in *La Juive*. After a few weeks at Hamburg, the contralto epoch began in April, 1868, at Berlin, where she made a promising début as Azucena and a still more emphatic success as Fidès. It was this display that led to her prolonged engagement at the Hofoper. For eighteen years, on and off, she remained there, appearing in every kind of rôle, not omitting the inevitable though certainly not contralto one, of Valentine!

She once related how nearly she had missed the opportunity of making her long career at Berlin. On her way she called upon a Berlin agent who was anxious to recommend another singer in her place. She told him she had been advised to sing for the Hamburg Intendant, and that he would be sure to take her. He then asked her to sing for him, and, when she had finished, said: "Dear child, you shall not go to Hamburg. I engage you for Berlin." She was thunderstruck, but he sent her to the manager of the Royal Opera, and on the afternoon of the same day she had in her pocket a three years' contract, at an honorarium of 1800 thalers the first year, 2000 the second, 3000 the third.

2

Such was the versatile and accomplished artist who returned to London to take part in the Pollini-Franke campaign of 1882. She found herself vis-à-vis of a public vastly changed from that which had treated her with indifference ten years before.

Unfortunately we still heard less of Marianne Brandt than we ought to have done. She only appeared a few times altogether in her renowned impersonations of Brangäne, Fidelio, and Ortrud. I recollect it being stated that she was out of voice during her stay in London. One critic declared that her voice was not so fresh as it had been. Another had it that she was "put in the shade" by her younger rival, Thérèse Malten. Be this as it may, she presented to us, on the first production of *Tristan* in England, the classical model for the rôle of Brangäne, an embodiment of irresistible charm and power, which was afterwards imitated and perhaps in some respects equalled, but never surpassed.

But the real truth was that the singer was constantly in an anxious and discontented frame of mind, wanting to break off her engagment here and get away to Bayreuth. For in the following July *Parsifal* was to be performed for the first time, and was in active rehearsal during the very month (June) when the German opera season was going on in London. Marianne Brandt had been asked by Wagner to share the part of Kundry with Materna and Thérèse Malten ; but she had a sort of feeling that, were she to be on the spot soon enough, she might stand a chance of *creating* it. That, of course, was not to be ; for Wagner had expressly requested Materna to be the first Kundry, and there she was, perfectly well and in possession, taking part in the preparations at Bayreuth.

As matters turned out, Fräulein Brandt lost nothing through being held in reserve for the second performance. Her impersonation was admired for its originality and for the fulness that her rich chest tones enabled her to impart to Kundry's lower music. In London her high notes may not have pleased, but they did everywhere else, including New York, where the greatest all-round triumphs of her career were soon to be achieved. Those triumphs, coming after two years more of hard work at Berlin, confirmed the opinion of Mme Pauline Viardot-Garcia, with whom she had studied during a couple of summers at Baden-Baden, and from whom she had learnt among other things her magnificent Fidès.

The illustrious singer and teacher had said to her in effect—" I was myself capable of singing any rôle but those written for a light soprano. You, with your astonishing compass, have the same gift. Sing any music you like, so long as you do not have to tire or force your voice ". Evidently she took Mme Viardot at her word, and, what was more, she demonstrated beyond cavil her ability to apply the same test to Wagner without injuring her voice in the slightest degree.

From Fidelio to Fricka and Fidès, from Maddalena in *Rigoletto* to Magdalena in *Die Meistersinger*, from

Elvira to Amneris, from Erda to Eglantine in *Euryanthe*, from Brangäne to Wellgunde and Ortrud—in these and a dozen other parts she gave amazing proofs of her versatility during the years that she sang in America. She became a great favourite there in course of what proved to be the closing period of her active career. To the end, in 1890, she remained one of the acknowledged mistresses of her art, one of the most talented and capable of the distinguished Wagnerian singers who helped to spread the master's fame and win his cause in two hemispheres. Then she retired to her native city of Vienna and for several years did admirable work as a teacher.

∧

III. ROSA SUCHER

I

This delightful artist was my first Isolde, my first Eva, and my first Euryanthe. In these three characters she appeared at Drury Lane during the Pollini-Franke season of 1882. Neither *Tristan* nor *Die Meistersinger* had been previously heard in this country; while Weber's opera counted merely as an interesting revival and relapsed, I fear, into its wonted oblivion. But the reader will readily imagine the state of excitement prevailing among Wagner-lovers when the opportunity at last arrived for hearing in their entirety the two great works whereof, for four years, we had had to be content with nibbling the tantalizing snippets· given at the Richter Concerts.

It was an immense satisfaction to us all to know that we were to witness these stage performances under the bâton of the same eminent conductor who had been our mentor and guide; who had been Wagner's "right-hand man" at Bayreuth and was still the darling of the Viennese musical "gods". Under tutelage such as Richter's the readings and the interpretation were bound to be right. The rest depended upon the artists, most of whom were known to the London public by reputation only. It must be borne in mind that the best of the available Bayreuth singers were at that moment touring in Angelo Neumann's company, which we had already been hearing a month

before in the *Ring*.[1] At the head of the Drury Lane
list stood the name of " Frau Rosa Sucher, Prima
Donna, Hamburgh Opera House ".

Rosa Hasselbeck was the daughter of a schoolmaster and choir-trainer living at Velburg (Bavaria).
Her father began teaching her when she was quite
young, and made her one of the soloists in his choir
at the parish church. She was only fourteen when,
taking part in a mass at some festival, the bright, full
tones of the girl soprano drew attention to her
uncommon gifts. Soon afterwards her father died,
and she went to live with relations.

In 1871, having attained her 22nd year and her voice
having developed magnificently, she resolved to
obtain a hearing from the Intendant of the Hofoper
at Munich. So delighted was he with her rendering
of Agathe's great air, " Leise, leise ", from *Der
Freischütz*, that he forthwith engaged her to sing
small parts, thus enabling her at the same time to
pursue her studies. Ere long she made her début at
Trier, where her success led to a two years' engagement at Königsberg, followed by some brilliant
appearances at Kroll's Theatre, Berlin. In 1876 she
met Joseph Sucher, a composer and conductor of the
Leipzig Stadttheater, who engaged her not only to
sing at his theatre but to marry him as well.

Their union proved an exceptionally happy one,
and the career of Rosa Sucher began to open out. Her

---

[1] I was still a rather youthful journalist to be the musical
critic of the *Sunday Times*, to which post I had been appointed
some few months previously. My personal experience of opera
abroad was then chiefly limited to France, Belgium and Italy ;
my wanderings in Germany, Austria, etc., not having begun so
early as 1882.

ROSA SUCHER

fame spread all through Germany, more particularly on account of her ever-growing powers as an exponent of Wagner's earlier heroines. Pollini, of Hamburg, went to hear her, and found in her the ideal artist for romantic and emotional characters. But man and wife were not to be separated; he had to engage them both; nor did he have occasion to regret the venture. Sucher joined his wife at Hamburg in 1879, and they became tremendous favourites both there and at the Berlin Hofoper, where the singer remained until 1898.

2

Frau Sucher's début as Elsa, on the opening night of the London season of 1882, was inscribed long ago among the red-letter events of my operatic experience. I had already heard some good Elsas in course of the seven years that *Lohengrin* had been in the repertory here. But neither before nor since has it been my lot to behold anyone so absolutely perfect in the part as this Bavarian representative of the Brabantian maiden. And to say " perfect " in this instance is to mean that we were witnessing for the first time the ideal histrionic realization of Wagner's conception. Until then we had never truly understood the character.

To analyze it at length would take too much space. From first to last this Elsa seemed to be under a hypnotic spell; while the fact that her face was so beautiful in its expression of maiden-like innocence enhanced our feeling of pity at her suffering and humiliation as she faced her accusers. At the moment of her entry, advancing without perceptible bodily movement, she almost gave the impression of being a somnambulist in a dream. In this new aspect scene after scene cleared away all the apparent inconsistencies of Elsa's character—her inability to resist the baleful influence of Ortrud, her passionless response to Lohengrin's pleading, her unheeding impulse to learn his name at any cost. Then, besides her enchanting beauty and her dramatic power, the gifted artist exercised over us another and no less inescapable charm—a lovely voice allied to complete mastery of the vocal art. Imagine the joy of hearing Wagner's still-unhackneyed melodies and his even more unfamiliar text from the lips of such an exquisite singer! Even the anti-Wagnerites melted and the harsh Bayreuth critics altered their tone.[1]

Similar rare qualities in her Senta and Elisabeth, which followed, evoked a growing admiration for her art. The more one heard of her voice the more one loved it for its haunting musical timbre and the sweet, human tenderness of its pure *cantilena*. The Prayer in *Tannhäuser* became an actual revelation, coming as it did after the most dramatic rendering (with great singers like Winkelmann as Tannhäuser and Gura as Wolfram) of the ensemble in the second act that we in London had heard up to that time. Indeed, Hans Richter was wont to declare his belief that no finer Elisabeth than Rosa Sucher had ever adorned the lyric stage.

After this came the two most notable events of the season, *viz.*, the first performances in England of *Die*

---

[1] For example, *The Morning Post* :

In the part of Elsa, Frau Rosa Sucher was so far superior to all the rest of the *dramatis personæ* that the greater share of public favour was distinctly her due, inasmuch as the hearts of the whole of the assembly were won by her most beautiful, artistic, and sympathetic performance.

Meistersinger and *Tristan and Isolde*, on May 30th and June 20th respectively. Frau Sucher enacted the heroine in each, therewith providing a contrast of styles—veritable *chefs-d'œuvre* of Comedy and Tragedy —such as our then-recent bowing acquaintance with the *Ring* could alone have prepared us adequately to appreciate. For my own part, I would say that her Eva was an exquisite combination of Ellen Terry's Beatrice and Portia, and I leave it at that.

Her Isolde stood in the foreground of a representation thrice memorable to the writer because it completed his conversion to the cause of Richard Wagner. The cast comprised, in addition, Marianne Brandt as Brangäne, Winkelmann as Tristan, Gura as König Marke, and Kraus as Kurwenal; with, of course, Richter conducting—a wonderful ensemble. Rosa Sucher proved to be the Isolde of our dreams, a fact the more marvellous then, as it seemed, because the rôle reflected her genius in a wholly fresh light. Until that night, as the critic of the *Post* pointed out, she had had " little opportunity for the display of other than what may be called the passive emotions. As Isolde her acting is full of active passion ; and at times it rose to the height of tragedy. The love passages were beautiful and tender, and the final scene few in the theatre could witness unmoved ".

Little more need be said. I only once met this charming woman, though I saw her in after years at Bayreuth, where she sang Isolde in '86 and Eva and Kundry in '88 ; also once at Berlin, where I had the opportunity to hear her sing the part of Venus in *Tannhäuser*. In 1892—the Mahler year—she paid another brief and final visit to London, appearing with success as the Brünnhilde of *Siegfried* and also as

Isolde. Three years later she took part in New York, under the bâton of Anton Seidl, in a season of German Opera organized by Walter Damrosch. But she did not stay in America long. In November, 1903, she took her final farewell of the stage at the Hofoper as Sieglinde in *Die Walküre*. Her death occurred in the same city in 1927, when she was in her 79th year.

IV. THERESE VOGL

Old Bayreuth pilgrims can generally remember the names of the singers they have heard in *The Ring* or *Parsifal* or *Tristan*. I wonder, though, how many Wagner-lovers of to-day could say off-hand who first sang the part of Brünnhilde on the stage in London. As a matter of fact, it was that very distinguished artist Therese Vogl, one of the greatest of all the early Wagnerian sopranos and, for certain reasons, the one whose name seems to be most in danger of becoming forgotten in this country. For unfortunately her stay here was exceedingly brief—just long enough for her to grace the original cycles of the tetralogy at Her Majesty's Theatre, that was all; and even then as Brünnhilde only in the first cycle, as Sieglinde in the second. She never visited us again.

Another point is that midway in her career she and her gifted husband, Heinrich Vogl, quarrelled with the Wagners and ceased to take part in the Bayreuth Festspiel. After that it did not take long for the Vogls to retire into the background, and suffer the indifference that accompanies forgetfulness and ingratitude. There is no need to enter into details here. But the memory of the artistry remains green, and I am among those who are thankful ever to have heard so great an artist as Therese Vogl. It was to be regretted that she could not appear in London as Isolde. She was then the most renowned of all Isoldes, and it would have been delightful beyond measure to compare her with Rosa Sucher. Heinrich Vogl was practically the original representative of Tristan in 1865 and for several years reckoned to be the *only* Tristan. It was the privilege of those who went to Munich in the 70's to see husband and wife together in Wagner's immortal love-tragedy. It must have been a glorious experience.

The pair appeared in London together under Seidl's bâton in the *Ring*, he in his original part of Loge (as well as that of Siegfried), she as Brünnhilde ; whilst Niemann, the famous tenor, despite his somewhat worn voice, could still declaim magnificently enough to impress us in his original rôle of Siegmund. It must be confessed that the unique opportunity of hearing these and other Bayreuth " creators " was hardly appreciated at its full value either by public or critics. The latter were obsessed by the immensity of the work and could not find time or space to write about its interpreters, whom they did not regard quite in the light of singers. An exception, perhaps, was furnished by Dr Hueffer of *The Times ;* but even he dwelt little upon the purely vocal side of things.

My own recollection of Frau Vogl's voice is that it was of a calibre similar to Christine Nilsson's—a light rather than a heavy dramatic soprano—and possessing the same exceptional clarity and resonance in the head register. It was this, combined with her easy production and her elegant phrasing and diction, that made her such an admirable exponent of a declamatory method which was then virtually new to English listeners.

She was supremely fine in *Götterdämmerung*, and notably thrilling in the closing scene ; though not more so than I had thought Materna when she sang the concert excerpt of the same scene, with Wagner seated beside her, at the Albert Hall five years before. Let me add, however, that there were many, like myself, of the opinion that the beauty and passion of Frau Vogl's singing as Sieglinde—the reflex, no doubt, of her wonderful Isolde—eclipsed her own effort in the love duet with Siegfried. And, by the way, it was she who created the part of Sieglinde at Munich, where it still remains as precious a tradition as her Isolde.

Alike by birth, education, and musical training, she was a thorough Bavarian. Born November 12th, 1845, at the little town of Tutzing, on Lake Starnberg, Therese Thoma (her maiden name) studied at the Munich Conservatoire and made her début at the Carlsruhe Stadttheater in 1865. A year later she sang for the first time at Munich in Auber's comic opera *La Part du Diable*,[1] a bright, tuneful work then very popular in Paris. Her reception was wholly favourable, but the opinions expressed regarding the rich quality of her medium notes induced her teacher, Hauser, to turn her attention to dramatic soprano rôles. In this way her fitness for operas of the romantic school gradually became manifest and, as we have seen, she developed into a Wagnerian singer of the highest order. She married in 1868 and died at Munich September 29th, 1921, surviving her husband by twenty years.

[1] *La Part du Diable* well deserves revival. The libretto, by Scribe, is written around the famous singer, Farinelli, who is represented by a woman, and whose sister, Casilda, is the character that Fräulein Thoma undertook.

V. HEDWIG REICHER-KINDERMANN

This was London's first Fricka and second Brünnhilde. A beautiful woman as well as a beautiful singer, she made it easy for us to comprehend her ascendancy over Wotan. Her scolding and her reproaches had the quality of seeming thoroughly merited; she aroused our sympathy for the outraged wife instead of compelling us—like so many of the unattractive Frickas (until Olczewska) who came after her—to waste our pity on the henpecked god. On the other hand, when this same fascinating personage played the erring Valkyrie, our feelings were reversed. Every bit of sympathy went out in advance to the disobedient Brünnhilde, and we decided that ten minutes of Fricka's curtain-lecture had been more than enough.

Hedwig Reicher-Kindermann was a native of Munich, now in her 29th year, and she had been something of a prodigy. When barely halfway through her teens she went on the stage of the Royal Opera House as one of the apprentices in *Die Meistersinger*; but her real début occurred in operetta at the Gärtnerplatz, where she met her future husband, the actor Reicher. She had been the first singer to attain celebrity as a Wagner heroine along this precise line; perhaps also the first who could claim to have sung Erda at Bayreuth in 1876 and yet be coming to London to enact Fricka and Brünnhilde.

The historic tour of Europe organized by Angelo

REICHER-KINDERMANN AS BRÜNNHILDE

Neumann for the exploitation of the *Ring* had begun at Berlin, and several other German cities had been visited. Full rehearsals in London being therefore unnecessary, we were deprived of a chance of closer acquaintance with the colossal work we were all longing to hear. On the opening night everyone was intensely excited and abnormally punctual. You could have heard a pin drop when the lights went down and the deep boom of the *Rheinmotiv* began its prolonged " hum " low down in the basses. That was a great moment for the starved Wagnerites of heathenish London; nor was it really easy for a youthful critic to collect his scattered thoughts sufficiently to weigh the merits of the strange artists engaged in the presentation of the famous music-drama.

But I remember very distinctly the heroic face, form, and figure, the commanding voice and manner, of the regal personage who awoke Wotan from sleep and bade him attend to the business of the day. I remember still more vividly how, on the following night, she drove her chariot and pair (of rams) into the rocky glen where Wotan has an appointment with his daughter, and how majestically she lashed her errant husband into obedience and submission. That superb Fricka, resolute and irresistible to the last degree, was Hedwig Reicher-Kindermann. I can confess now that, when she had finished and taken her departure, I was truly sorry; for I knew that, during the remainder of the colossal music-drama, we were to see Fricka no more.

I am not sure that the critics were invited to the second cycle; I rather fancy not. But I know that I went and sat out every note of it, learning more and more of the music, and otherwise richly rewarded by seeing and hearing the fascinating Fricka of the first cycle as the Brünnhilde of this one. She came out of the ordeal remarkably well, suffering little, if at all, by the inevitable comparison with Frau Vogl, who now changed over from Brünnhilde to Sieglinde. In the estimation of Anton Seidl, Hedwig was a genius. But what might have been an exceptionally brilliant career was unhappily cut short in the following summer, whilst the company was at Trieste. There Hedwig Reicher-Kindermann died suddenly on June 2nd, within a few weeks of her thirtieth birthday, to the profound regret of all who had heard her.

VI. THÉRÈSE MALTEN

Thérèse Malten was another of the great German sopranos whose happy lot it was, in the early days of the Crusade, to aid in bringing the gospel of Wagner to the English stage. At Dresden hers was a name to conjure with. To the music-loving Saxons she was something of a divinity; for they looked upon her as their own. Until her début there in 1873 she had never been on the operatic stage. She came to them a completely-trained singer and actress; a fully-fledged *Künstlerin*, good enough to start with no less a part than Pamina in the *Zauberflöte* and carry off all the honours. So they simply adored her and took care never to let her go again—for long.

She was not, however, a Dresdener by birth. Her native town was Insterburg, in E. Prussia, and most of her early life she had spent in Danzig, where her father held a military post. Her advanced studies took the family to Berlin, where she worked for three years at the Hochschule and also under the actor Richard Kahle. To their teaching and her patience in biding her time was due her instant success at Dresden.

In the late seventies she won laurels at home and abroad in the earlier Wagner operas, and then the master himself heard her, with results that became manifest to the world in her great year—1882. First she went to London to take a prominent part in the

German season at Drury Lane, and next to Bayreuth, invited by Wagner to share with Materna and Marianne Brandt the rôle of Kundry. She was not quite thirty and had only been on the stage nine years.

It was in *Fidelio*, on the night of Queen Victoria's birthday, that Thérèse Malten made her English début. Hearing her for the first time, I could not quite make up my mind whether I liked her head notes or not. They did not sound so round and full as the medium,—rather a drawback, I thought, in a dramatic soprano. Afterwards we were informed that she had been out of voice and ought not to have sung. In course of a few nights she gave eloquent proof of this in parts like Elsa, Elisabeth, and Eva, alternating therein with the redoubtable Rosa Sucher.

Short as her stay was, it sufficed to enable us to " correct our bearings ", while some of us, who subsequently witnessed her superb impersonation of Kundry at Bayreuth, formed an even more exalted estimate of her gifts.[1] She was certainly very wonderful in the part; so completely satisfying in every respect that in 1884 she was chosen to undertake it away from Bayreuth on two notable occasions. One of these was a private stage performance of *Parsifal* given at Munich before the mad King Ludwig of Bavaria; the other, a recital of the work in concert form for the first time in London, given at the Albert Hall on November 10

[1] Really it was impossible not to feel a certain measure of sympathy for Wagner in his *embarras de choix* where Kundry was concerned. First Materna, then Marianne Brandt, then Thérèse Malten—his admiration for all three about equal; and each in turn made a brilliant success in the part. Still, he only lived to see *Parsifal* through the Festival of 1882. By the following summer he was dead, and the " embarrassment of choice " had devolved upon his widow and son.

A

(and repeated five days later), under the direction of Joseph Barnby.

The latter event aroused extraordinary curiosity. For at that date *Parsifal* was not alone a sacred drama, but a drama sacred to Bayreuth; we had heard no more of it than a few excerpts played at the Richter Concerts. Once more, after a lapse of seven years, was the huge auditorium at Kensington the scene of what was for London a Wagnerian revelation—with " maimed rites ", truly, but nevertheless of absorbing interest. The performance had been carefully rehearsed, and altogether, having regard to the newness and difficulty of the music, it reflected great credit upon the Albert Hall choir and orchestra, and also the conductor to whose initiative the whole venture was due.

Speaking of the Kundry, Dr Hueffer wrote in *The Times :* " Fräulein Malten especially evoked a perfect storm of enthusiasm by a voice of the exceptional range required by Wagner, which she, moreover, produces with ease and purity ". Three months before that he had written from Bayreuth, " One night the audience admire the inimitable grace and rare beauty of voice of Fräulein Malten as Kundry, while on the next they are impressed by the dramatic fire of Frau Materna ". The present writer had the good fortune to hear both in the part, and can recall that, although the two Kundrys differed little in conception or treatment, one detail of Malten's stood out as individual and unique. That was in the second act, in the episode where Klingsor summons her to his castle and awakens her out of her hypnotic sleep to aid him in the seduction of Parsifal. The thrill of those piteous cries of lamentation—the moaning and misery, or *Jammer*, as the Germans call it, when Kundry returns to the consciousness of her enslavement to the dread sorcerer—unearthly and terrible, yet not ugly or repellent as they were, can never be forgotten by anyone who heard Malten in this scene.

The last time she appeared in London was in 1886, when she came over with Herr Gudehus to sing at the Richter Concerts in two important Wagner selections, *viz.*, the second act of *Tristan* and the last act of *Siegfried*. On both occasions she sang magnificently, Mr (now Sir George) Henschel being also in the cast; but the attendance at the second concert was so meagre that the experiment resulted in a heavy loss.

VII. LILLI LEHMANN

That musical talent runs in families has been shown
again and again in the course of this book. Lilli
Lehmann's mother had been an opera singer at Cassel
and a first-rate harpist; a friend of Spohr, in whose
operas she sang and many of whose harp compositions
she used to play in public. When her career ended she
settled down temporarily as a vocal teacher at Würz-
burg in Bavaria, where, on May 15th, 1848, her
daughter Lilli was born. Together with her sister
Lilli became her mother's pupil and, it is said,
studied the technique of her art with no one else.
She must have had a good teacher, for in this instance
nature, environment, and education combined to
produce a very wonderful woman.

She was in her eighteenth year when she made her
first essay upon the operatic stage at Prague, replacing
someone as the First Boy in Mozart's *Zauberflöte*.
For a time she went on earning her experience in
operas, operettas, plays, and farces; next at Danzig,
singing 18 or 20 times a month in *coloratura* and
soubrette parts; later on at Leipzig and at the Berlin
Hofoper, where she made her début as Vielka in
Meyerbeer's *Feldlager in Schlesien*. She remained one of
Berlin's favourites—hardly less popular as a light
soprano than was her contemporary, Pauline Lucca,
in her line.

A light soprano—precisely; and in view of her

subsequent career what an interesting fact! We have here something which differentiates Lilli Lehmann's career entirely from the common development traced hitherto in the lives of the heroines of these pages ; the very reverse, for example, of Patti and Lucca, who were Valentinas and Leonoras practically in their teens. Natures vary; and it can only be accepted as a general rule that it is safer for a young opera singer to begin with light parts and gradually work into the heavier ones. But the point in Lilli Lehmann's case is that at Berlin the Intendant definitely stamped and hall-marked her as a *soprano sfogato* or *soprano leggiero*—a *Coloratursängerin* pure and simple—and denied her the privilege of trying her hand at anything else. It was the fashion of the time; but time was to prove that in this instance Baron von Hülsen had made a mistake.

Every year with Lilli Lehmann was a year of progress. Whilst adding rôle after rôle to her special repertoire she was constantly working to strengthen her voice and extend the scope of her art. Talk of her talent had reached Bayreuth long before the opening of the new theatre. Wagner selected her as one of his three Rhine-daughters for the inaugural performance in 1876; also as Helmwige, the Valkyrie, and to sing the music of the Forest-bird in *Siegfried*. This experience was so successful that it encouraged her to persevere with her quiet preparation for a career in Wagnerian and heavier parts generally. Among these she took a tremendous liking for Norma, and in course of time it was to prove one of her finest rôles.

In many respects she somewhat resembled Tietjens. Both stood rather above medium height; both were classical and statuesque in their gestures and supremely fine actresses. Tietjens had the heavier voice, but in beauty of quality and carrying power there was a distinct similarity to be noted. Both possessed the same rare faculty for investing their Italian *fiorituri* —in " Casta diva " for instance—with dramatic significance as well as mere brilliancy. Their Mozart singing was of the purest type. If Tietjens was the ideal Donna Anna, Lilli Lehmann was the no less perfect Constanze in *Die Entführung;* their Leonora in *Fidelio* also stood upon the same exalted level; and I can make these comparisons because I heard both artists.

Lilli Lehmann profited physically by the very restrictions that limited her to lighter parts during her 15 years at Berlin. Fortunately for her, she did not become a dramatic soprano during Wagner's lifetime, or he would probably have given her strenuous work in his music-dramas before her organ had the requisite stamina. She belonged to the class that he stipulated for in his Bayreuth period—the singer with an old-fashioned Italian training. It was still this healthy equipment that she exhibited on the occasion of her first visit to London in the summer of 1880, when she made a " promising " début as Violetta in *La Traviata* at Her Majesty's.

That success she followed up with another as Filina in *Mignon,* the cast including Christine Nilsson, Trebelli, Campanini, and Del Puente. But it was not yet the fully-expanded Lilli Lehmann whom we heard then, though one critic took the opportunity to indulge the comforting reflection that " When one of the Bayreuth Festival artists is found at a London opera-house singing such a part as Filina, whose *raison d'être* is that she may deliver brilliant arias in contrast to the more touching music of *Mignon*, it becomes evident that the power of melody continues to assert itself ".

2

Three or four years later there was a season of German opera at Covent Garden, under the conductorship of Dr Hans Richter. The company did not boast an Isolde and for a time it seemed probable that the long-awaited revival of Wagner's *Tristan* would fail to materialize. Then the unexpected happened. It was announced that the work would be placed in rehearsal and the part of the heroine undertaken by the *ci-devant* light soprano, Fräulein Lilli Lehmann.

The explanation of her coming was simple. She had determined to prove that, whatever her Intendant might insist upon at Berlin, she could be what she chose and sing what rôles she fancied anywhere else *during her holiday*. This step ultimately proved to be the turning point in her career. Her triumph in London as Isolde established her position and fame as a Wagnerian soprano in the eyes of the whole musical world.[1]

[1] As evidence of this I cannot do better than quote from the highly laudatory notice written in *The Times* by Dr Francis Hueffer. He said (July 7, 1884) :

The question frequently started whether *Tristan* or *Die Meistersinger* is in itself a more perfect thing is one of personal idiosyncrasy rather than of personal reasoning. . . . Whether *Die Meistersinger* will outlive *Tristan* or *vice-versâ*, whether both or either will survive the changes of time and taste—these and similar questions may safely be left to the period from which Wagner's music derives its name—the future.

The greatest weakness of the German troupe (at Covent Garden) has hitherto been the want of a soprano able to grapple

This unequivocal triumph in an outstanding rôle like Isolde encouraged the artist not only to extend her Wagner répertoire, but to obtain recognition from Baron von Hülsen of her right to attempt the heavier characters at the Berlin Hofoper where she had been singing for fifteen years. Whilst the matter stood in abeyance, she obtained leave of absence in the autumn of 1885 for her first visit to America, and made her début at the Metropolitan in November, Anton Seidl conducting. There her success was so emphatic that she was induced to prolong her stay beyond the limit of her furlough and to accept further engagements for musical festivals at Cincinnati and Milwaukee. The Baron's angry protests passed unheeded; his fine of 13,000 marks was promptly paid; only, when Lilli wanted to sing at Kroll's Theatre in Berlin, his permission was obstinately withheld.

The consequence of this split was an estrangement that lasted until 1890. During the interval she sang for months every year at New York, in addition to earning a great reputation at Bayreuth with her magnificent assumptions of Isolde and Brünnhilde.

---

with the vocal and dramatic requirements of Wagner's heroines. This deficiency can no longer be said to exist after the appearance of Fräulein Lehmann as Isolde. As a singer, this lady would adorn any stage; as an actress she has few equals, even among the artists trained in Wagner's school. Her rich and sonorous voice is managed with consummate skill, and her intonation is perfect. As a piece of mere vocalization her share in the great duet of the second act, as well as the death-song, may challenge comparison with anything at present to be heard on the London stage. As a dramatic representation, her Isolde was worthy of even higher praise. The blonde Irish maiden, full of passion and death-defying heroism, was realized by her in all the various aspects which music and poetry have given to the character.

She was now about forty years of age, and her superb organ—her "luscious voice, velvety as Patti's", as Wagner had once described it—was in its prime. She furnished London with a favourable opportunity for judging of this fact in June, 1887. She had recently married a well-known German tenor, Paul Kalisch, who did *not* appear with her on her *rentrée* at Her Majesty's in *Fidelio* (the Florestan on that occasion being M. Caylus). Subsequently, however, they sang together in Beethoven's opera (given in Italian), and in each instance made us regret that such a glorious Leonora should not have had better support.

Lilli Lehmann had made a close and exhaustive study of this rôle.[1] Comparisons between her and Tietjens were inevitable, for in 1887 Tietjens had only been dead ten years; yet the new Leonora suffered little by them. Neither, on the other hand, did her embodiment receive the careful analysis and criticism that it deserved. For my own part I can say that I was immensely struck by the grandeur and nobility of her dramatic conception, by the ease with which she rose superior to her entourage, and, above all, her vivid realization of that "inner spirit" of the character, upon which she placed even greater importance than the actual singing of the music. Nevertheless her delivery of the "Abscheulicher" has remained among the most beautiful and impressive —so "full of deep tragic intensity and yearning" was it—that I have ever listened to. Her performance as a whole revealed not merely new power, but the expanding genius of an extraordinary artist.

[1] As she was to demonstrate further in an admirable little book, *Studie zu Fidelio*, published by Breitkopf und Härtel.

3

Another long interval—twelve years this time of hard work in America and her native land, where she had become *persona gratissima*—elapsed before she paid her next and final visit to London, to give a magnificent display in full maturity of her greatest characters. It never has been and never will be forgotten by opera-goers who enjoyed the rich treat afforded during those few weeks in June and July, 1899. She appeared in six of her finest delineations, *viz.*, Leonora, Donna Anna, Norma, Ortrud, Isolde, and Sieglinde; and did so in worthy company. Indeed, the more eminent her compeers, the stronger the light amid which her own gifts stood out in what seemed very like kaleidoscopic epitome of her artistic life-work.

The most remarkable of the features of the display were its versatility and its all-round *maestria ;* and to indicate these I will briefly repeat here a few lines from my own criticism of each assumption :

(1) " Mme. Lilli Lehmann is still a great Fidelio ; and notwithstanding the signs of wear and tear now becoming apparent in her medium register, the voice still retains so much of its freshness and power that one can listen with pleasure to her artistic and expressive rendering of Beethoven's immortal music. . . . The dramatic side of the performance, however, still remains an achievement of supreme excellence, replete with pathetic grandeur, tragic force and intensely touching sentiment ".

(2) " Mme. Lilli Lehmann was the Sieglinde, and here surely we had for once the ideal embodiment of a part that many sopranos undertake and scarcely any understand. . . . She solves the problem of that wonderful first act to an extent that perhaps only one or two Sieglindes have yet achieved ".

(3) " It was the first time that Mme. Lilli Lehmann had treated us to her noble and impressive impersonation of Donna Anna, and whilst to some it came as a revelation of tragic grandeur and vocal beauty, to others of longer experience it recalled with singular closeness the ample tones and broad dignified style of Theresa Tietjens. Certainly never since Tietjens have the lyric boards of this metropolis seen a Donna Anna to be compared with Lilli Lehmann ".

(4) " She is quite great enough in the part of Norma to warrant the revival of an opera which, in all but undying melodic beauty, now seems hopelessly out of date. She presents a wonderfully dignified yet pathetic embodiment of the erring priestess, and rises in the fullest degree to the tragic situation of the last act. . . . Her rendering of ' Casta diva ' was in many ways quite untraditional, being sung for the greater part in a delicate *mezza-voce* that suggested in a striking degree the idea of mystery and awe ".

(5) " The music of Ortrud was written primarily for a mezzo-soprano, and many of its important passages lie in a part of the voice where Mme. Lehmann is utterly unable to cope with the sonorous undercurrent of the Wagner orchestra. She not only atoned largely for this deficiency by the splendid ringing quality of her high notes, but sang throughout with rare breadth of style and unfailing intelligence ".

(6) " Her Isolde . . . is immeasurably superior to the average in virtue of the rare vocal and histrionic attributes that raise Mme. Lehmann high above the ordinary level. . . . It was in the last scene of all that she impressed most profoundly. It was then that the great tragic actress, rising to the full height of a sublime situation, touched every heart as never in my experience had audience been touched by this climax of Wagner's moving Drama ".[1]

[1] The casts of the above representations were with one exception remarkable ; and as usual, it was *Fidelio* that failed, as a whole, to receive its just due—even with Dr Muck in the

By now she had finished her career in America,
where I met her in New York in 1896 at the house of
her friend, Henry Krehbiel. I found her an extraordinarily interesting woman, but inclined to be
rather severe in her judgment of other artists and their
vocal methods. She was already thinking about her
book on singing, which she brought out in Berlin
(in 1900) whilst teaching there shortly before her final
retirement from the stage. From what Krehbiel
afterwards said in his *Chapters of Opera*, I gathered
that she had once felt little admiration for the De
Reszkes and Lassalle (" they were fine men, but they
needed to study more "). But when the Polish
brothers took to singing in German and she was
appearing with them in London her opinion changed;
she thought there were no greater artists to be heard.
In short, her own standard was perfection; and she
demanded no less from all opera singers who professed
to work upon similar lines.

conductor's seat. In *Die Walküre*, Nordica was the Brünnhilde,
Van Dyck the Siegmund, David Bispham the Wotan, and
Olitzka the Fricka. In *Don Giovanni* there were Scotti, Edouard
de Reszke, Journet, Gilibert, Salignac, Nordica, and Zélie de
Lussan. In *Norma*, Giulia Ravogli, Dippel, and Plançon. In
Lohengrin, Jean de Reszke, Edouard de Reszke, Bispham, and
Nordica. Finally, in *Tristan*, Jean and Edouard de Reszke,
Bispham, and Olitzka.

VIII. KATHARINA KLAFSKY

I

This remarkable soprano made her London début in the company of Therese Vogl and Hedwig Reicher-Kindermann at Her Majesty's as one of the Rhine-maidens in *Rheingold* and as Waltraute in *Die Walküre*. Only on that occasion she was no more than a subordinate member of Neumann's troupe at Leipzig, where a few months before she had won her first success as Brangäne on the production of *Tristan und Isolde*. Her day was still to come. We in London could hardly foresee that this modest Rhine-daughter would, within a year, be the Brünnhilde; still less that ten years later she would be returning to England a famous Wagnerian soprano, to sing the foremost rôles in the modern répertoire under the direction of Gustav Mahler.

Hers had been a curious rise to eminence. Her father, an impecunious cobbler, carried on his trade at the village of St. Janos (Hungary), where she was born September 19th, 1855. When she was fifteen her mother died, and the home was broken up, her father marrying again. The Klafskys had been inclined to be musical; but Katharina's voice had not as yet developed, and she left her native place to seek her fortune elsewhere. She walked every mile of the road to Vienna, and was once reduced to such extremities that at the town of Oedenburg, on the way, she was compelled to beg for food and lodging.

KLAFSKY AS LEONORA ("FIDELIO")

The girl's courage and self-reliance were rewarded when she got to the capital ; though not until she had earned her living for a time as a nurserymaid. During that period her singing first attracted notice, and her master and mistress introduced her to the organist of the Elisabeth-Kirche, who gave her some lessons and procured for her an engagement in the chorus at the Vienna Komische Oper. This, again, led to her being taken by the conductor to Mme Marchesi, who is said to have taught her for a short time without payment.[1] Still she did not get on. Although she was now twenty, her voice appears to have been still backward. An offer of work in the chorus and small parts at the Salzburg opera-house was gladly accepted, and there in 1876 she obtained not only experience but her first husband, a merchant, who promptly took her off the stage.

But Katharina Klafsky was not precisely hungering for bliss in private life. Soon after the honeymoon she went to the Leipzig Theatre to sing for Angelo Neumann, who engaged her to undertake *comprimaria* parts. She quickly proved her ability to do better than that, and became a highly useful member of the company. This engagement lasted from 1876 until 1882. Then came the *Nibelungen* tour and London. She left as she had arrived, with no more than a bare mention of her name.

But when the leading place in the company became vacant, Neumann immediately selected her to fill it. So she remained with him at Leipzig for three years

---

[1] Strangely enough, the famous teacher took care to mention in her book the name of every singer of repute who had studied with her, but for some unknown reason, omitted that of Katharina Klafsky.

Q

longer before going on to a still more lucrative position at Hamburg, where she stayed—now an immense favourite with the public—until her departure for America in 1895. During that interval she came twice more to London and took to herself in turn a second and a third husband. The former was a baritone named Greve, who had sung frequently over here, and the latter the well-known conductor, Otto Lohse.

2

A rather tempestuous career, it must be allowed. And now let me add something about the fully-fledged artist who first appeared in England in her true light during the oft-mentioned season given by Sir Augustus Harris in '92. The German performances under Gustav Mahler were taking place at Drury Lane, the "polyglot" at Covent Garden. It was at the former house on a hot July night that Frau Klafsky made her *rentrée* in *Fidelio*, what time a repetition of *Lohengrin* was in progress on the other side of Bow Street. I devoted my entire evening to Beethoven's opera and considered it "a very notable performance, which revealed Herr Mahler in the guise of an original musical thinker", while the new Leonora was "an artist who distinctly proved her title to rank with the greatest of her tribe".

Two things stand out in my memory. Mahler's new and magnificent reading of the "Leonora" overture (No. 3) and the acting of Klafsky in the prison scene.[1] A few nights later a second triumph

[1] I wrote in the *Sunday Times* : " Frau Klafsky only recently had the misfortune to lose her husband. It will easily be understood, therefore, that the artist made her return to the

awaited her as the Brünnhilde of *Götterdämmerung*. Mahler had rehearsed with infinite care what proved to be in many respects a unique performance. He made so few cuts that it lasted from 7 o'clock till midnight, a starving audience remaining for the last note. He dispensed with the Norns, but restored the gorgeous scene for Brünnhilde and Waltraute (see *Schumann-Heink*). All the Bayreuth stars of the moment were in the cast. Was there ever a greater Siegfried than Alvary? I doubt it.

Klafsky sang, truly, like one inspired; like one, moreover, who had the gift of inspiring others. Her voice rang out like a clarion, matching those of Alvary and Heink in the great duets and rising to sublime heights of declamatory grandeur in the closing scene. Such pathos in that wail of anguish, " Siegfried . . . kennt mich nicht! ", such passionate abandonment in the episode of the attestation before the assembled vassals came to us like a revelation. " That was the real thing, eh ? " said Mahler to me in his broken English, when it was all over, " She is an extraordinary woman ! " And then, a night or two afterwards, her Elisabeth. No living artist could have brought out with greater beauty and truth the deep

stage under conditions which materially enhanced the trying nature of her task. She threw such deep pathos and intense emotional force into her embodiment that, to those aware of her bereavement, it appeared as though her outbursts of grief and her fit of sobbing at the climax of the prison scene were not assumed but real. Acting it was, though, and fine tragic acting into the bargain. As a singer Frau Klafsky may now be considered in her prime. Her voice, of sympathetic timbre and admirably produced, is perfectly fresh and remarkably even in quality throughout. It expresses with wonderful variety every shade of powerful sentiment ".

poetic sentiment and pathos of the character. It was a singularly beautiful conception, carried out from first to last with wonderful delicacy and finish.[1]

In 1894 she was heard here for the last time, her third husband, Otto Lohse, being engaged to follow Mahler as conductor. By this time I had met her frequently and knew what a lively, vivacious disposition and fund of good humour lay behind the mask of seriousness which she assumed when on the stage. Her Greek profile and regular features, her piercing brown eyes, her height and massive build, the dignity of her carriage and gestures—all gave her a most imposing aspect in her heroic parts. Once out of her disguise, however, she was the simplest, jolliest creature imaginable, with a ready joke on the tip of her tongue. When she introduced me to Herr Lohse, she laughingly presented herself as " Leonora " and her husband as " No. 3 ", adding with a wink, " Stimmt, nit wahr ? " The poor man—an admirable conductor by the way—could say naught to the contrary.

She displayed her versatility that season by repeating the whole of the rôles she had sung two years previously, together with, in addition, Elsa, Isolde, and Agathe. She was amazingly good in all three, but her Isolde was especially fine. Her telling voice

---

[1] The *Tannhäuser* cast was worth recalling, since it was phenomenal even for the nineties. In addition to Klafsky, it included Avary as the hero ; the celebrated Reichmann as Wolfram ; Wiegand as the Landgrave ; Landau as Walther ; an incomparable Venus in Bettaque ; and Schumann-Heink in the tiny rôle of the Shepherd ; with, last but not least, Gustav Mahler as conductor. This revival, which marked the termination of an unusually brilliant German season, also set the seal upon the fame of the Hungarian soprano in our midst.

answered the demands upon it with the utmost ease, while womanly tenderness and overwhelming passion were in turn stamped upon her delivery of the music.

Krehbiel has told in brief the story of what happened after her last fateful American visit: how Frau Klafsky had arrived " under a cloud ", because, following Lilli Lehmann's example, she had violated her contract with her Hamburg Intendant; then how she had effected a reconciliation by handing over to Pollini half her fees. " Her success in America was emphatic " and " she was re-engaged by Mr Damrosch to alternate with Mme Lehmann in the season of 1896–97 ". But *l'homme propose mais Dieu dispose.* She returned to Europe without having completely recovered from the effects of an injury to her head, caused by a fall of scenery and resulting in a slight fracture of the skull. She even sang again once or twice at Hamburg, making her final appearance there in *Fidelio* on September 11th, 1896. After that she underwent a " trephining operation ", which, however, proved unsuccessful, and on the 22nd of the same month she died.

Katharina Klafsky had been little more than twenty years on the stage when this deplorable tragedy put an end to her brilliant career.

IX. MILKA TERNINA

I

It used to be said that Bayreuth was the cradle of great Wagnerian vocal art, as well as of everything else appertaining to the cult of the *Meister*. For my own part I could never subscribe to this view. Bayreuth has always been rather the finishing school or, better still, what the university is to the ordinary educational establishment. As a matter of fact, the style which we now associate with the " school " had not been definitely formed when the earlier exponents of Wagnerian music-drama assembled to perform the *Nibelungering* and *Parsifal*. The men jointly responsible for it were Wagner himself and his four renowned conductors, Hermann Lévi, Hans Richter, Anton Seidl, and Felix Mottl. Once the method was established it spread rapidly over the whole of Germany and Austria. Singers went to Bayreuth only to imitate its best exemplars.

Facile princeps among the conductors in 1876 was Hermann Lévi, who, apart from his many summers at the Festspielhaus, was for 24 years chief conductor at Munich. All his distinguished colleagues of the baton had been to London long before he made up his mind to follow in their wake. He did so in 1895, directing a Beethoven-Wagner programme at Queen's Hall with a quiet skill and well-controlled power that delighted all present.[1] He brought with him as vocalist on this occasion a young Croatian soprano, who had for several years been a favourite at the Munich Court Opera and earned a considerable reputation as a delineator of the Wagner heroines. Her name was Milka Ternina.

Now a great deal had been expected of this singer, and, to be candid, she did not come up to general anticipation. The critics, after making due allowance for the disadvantages of a concert début, which can never be quite fair to a dramatic singer accustomed only to the stage, were not quite satisfied, and expressed their opinions with much reserve.[2]

2

Milka Ternina came of a well-to-do family living at Begizse (Croatia), where she was born December

---

[1] His reading of the *Tannhäuser* overture was much discussed. It differed from both Richter's and Mottl's, and it was hard to decide which of the three realized Wagner's intentions most closely. However, I thought it "an extremely picturesque and impressive performance". A year or two later Lévi's mind became affected and he had to give up public work. He died at Munich in 1900.

[2] Pursuing the same course, I wrote in the *Sunday Times*: "The high English pitch frequently upset her intonation and caused apparent inconvenience in the management of the registers. . . . Her deliver of Elisabeth's 'Greeting' had not enough warmth or impulse, nor can it be said that she rose more fully to the height of her theme in the 'Invocation' from *Fidelio*. Fräulein Ternina has a splendid voice and is a singer of remarkable intelligence, but it is evidently only in combination with her qualities as an actress that she can display these rare gifts in their true light. Next time she makes her appearance in London I trust it will be in the guise of an Isolde or a Brünnhilde".

19th, 1863. Left an orphan in her childhood, she was adopted by her uncle, a State Councillor, who received her in his home at Agram and gave her a good general education. She showed early signs of having a strong voice, and began to study singing under a local teacher at the age of twelve. Not until she was seventeen did her uncle send her to Vienna to be trained by Gänsbacher for two years at the Conservatorium. She mastered a number of operatic parts, in some of which she sang at Agram, in others at Leipzig, where she secured in 1883 her first formal engagement. Then, after valuable work at Graz and Bremen, she gradually made a prominent position for herself in the estimation of North German operagoers.

Munich was then the centre of the most important activities in the domain of the lyric drama. It offered the widest scope for the exercise of a rare all-round talent such as Ternina had developed. The Intendant of the Royal Opera secured her services for a period of nine years (1890–99) and made her his " bright particular star ". She also appeared at concerts, winning fresh admirers by her combined charm and intellectuality as a Lieder-singer. In 1896 she paid her first visit to America, where her success was unequivocal.

Chief interest, however, attaches to her début at Covent Garden in 1898, after the death of Sir Augustus Harris, when Maurice Grau was managing director for the Grand Opera Syndicate. Now it was that the genius of the real Ternina emerged in full glory ; and I think that very few of us were prepared for a display of such effulgence. *Tristan* had already been given once that season with Jean de Reszke and Nordica as the lovers, and it was repeated with Milka Ternina as the Isolde.

The art of the new soprano—the extraordinary warmth of her voice and the eloquence of her diction, combined with a suppressed passion, intense, burning, yet reticent, that lay bare the whole soul of the woman—yielded a novel and delightful experience. Personally I could not help feeling that this was, of all the great Isoldes I had heard, the most original in conception, the most pathetic and touching in its womanly qualities, the strongest in psychological force. Subsequent opportunities were to confirm not only the truth of my impression, but the fact that those peculiar traits were the predominant factors in each of Ternina's striking gallery of impersonations. In a word, she was unlike any of her contemporaries, and yet equal to the best of them in histrionic grandeur, whilst surpassing most of them in sheer purity of musical charm. No matter what the type of rôle, she proved herself in all a supreme artist.

Owing to the Whitsuntide holidays, the audience at this début was not a particularly representative one, and, what was worse, few of the leading critics were present. The press notices were consequently meagre and sparing in their eulogy of the new singer. Then something unusual happened. A distinguished Wagner-lover, who was also even then a distinguished author, took up his pen and wrote a glowing half-column letter to *The Daily Chronicle* under the heading, " A Great Lyrical Achievement ", eloquently informing a careless world what Ternina's Isolde was like. I will not disguise the fact that the writer was Mr George Moore, because he openly signed his letter. Nor will I deny that the undiluted praise of so well-informed an amateur critic was warmly welcomed by all who read it. He said *inter alia* :

"If I were condemned to a desert island, and were allowed to choose for my distraction one act of Wagner, I should not hesitate for one moment. My first choice—and I believe most people will agree with me—would be the first act of *Tristan*. . . . Shakespeare himself has not written an act more poignant, in which the genius of the actress is required more continuously at every moment for the portrayal of some fugitive but potential mood ; every moment demands all her art, whether with voice or with facial expression, or with gesture, the drama calls upon her and not for superficial or comedy emotion, but that essential emotion which lies about the roots of life. . . .

"I have seen at least two women sing and act the part so well that it seemed as if they had achieved all that human nature could achieve. . . . Where Sucher was a whirlwind, Mlle. Ternina was a woman, a sublimation of womanhood, it is true, but a woman whom Tristan could love. She was neither an ordinary woman nor a mere elemental force ; she was the Isolde who came from Ireland to wed King Mark, and she did drink the love potion in mistake for the death potion. . . .

"Though Jean de Reszke sang as well as he had ever sung in his life, it was Ternina who was called at the end of the third Act. Her name was shouted from different parts of the house, and I have never heard the prima donna called in preference to the tenor when Jean de Reszke was singing. The house seemed to awaken slowly to the fact that the spectacle of a perfect incarnation of Isolde was being achieved ".[1]

3

In the cycles of the *Ring* that followed and which, by the way, Frau Cosima Wagner attended, Ternina

[1] Reprinted by the kind permission of Mr George Moore.

took Sieglinde in alternation with Emma Eames and
Brünnhilde with Marie Brema and Nordica. In her
duet with Jean de Reszke in *Siegfried* her fine voice and
perfect assimilation of the true vocal with the Wagnerian method yielded every noble artistic effect of
which the scene is susceptible. Still more unusual
was the fact that, in the third cycle, *Götterdämmerung*
had to be omitted altogether because Ternina and
Nordica were both ill, and the music of this section
always lay too high for Marie Brema. So the opera-
house that night remained closed, the disappointment
of the public being shared by Wagner's widow, who
declared that " she did not object to the *Götterdämmerung* with ' cuts ' in London, though she would
regard them as high treason at Bayreuth ".

Ternina's final triumph that season was won in
Fidelio. Much was expected of her Leonora, and she
excelled our most confident hopes. Said Joseph
Bennett in the *Daily Telegraph :* " She had every mood
of Florestan's faithful spouse so to speak at her
fingers' ends. She sang throughout with superb
feeling and a degree of *abandon* that made her performance immensely impressive. . . . Her delivery of
the magnificent scena, ' Abscheulicher', was among
the finest achievements of the evening ".

This was her last appearance in London until 1900,
the season made notable by the production of Puccini's
Tosca with Ternina in the title-rôle. She proved no
less perfect as an Italian singer than as an interpreter
of Wagner and Beethoven, and the element of surprise
about the whole thing was delightful. Admirably
supported by De Lucia as Cavaradossi, by Scotti as
Scarpia (a memorable embodiment), and Gilibert as
the Sagrestano, she thrilled her audience—to quote

The Times—" as it is very rarely thrilled. Her style is that of the best Italian models of the past ".

Ternina's magnificent Tosca was unique in its picturesque beauty, its dramatic contrasts, its irresistible sweep of tragic intensity from climax to climax. "No other Tosca has ever approached Ternina's ". Such was Puccini's own verdict when I put the question to him the last time he came to London. He was about the least demonstrative Italian I ever came across, and his smiles were worth treasuring. But his face was simply "wreathed" in them when, at the end of the first performance of *Tosca*, he came before the curtain with Ternina on one side and Scotti on the other amid a veritable tempest of applause.

Although versatility was among her paramount gifts, it is not to be denied that some characters suited her better than others. For example, her strong personality seemed "wasted upon the pale, pathetic figure of Lohengrin's bride ". On the other hand, when she sang Ortrud she "made the character as distinctive as any she has sustained here, going through her share of the Minster scene with an energy that gave renewed interest to a part that Tietjens did not deem unworthy a great artist ". That Elisabeth was her favourite may be inferred from the fact that she regularly chose it for her *rentrée* at Covent Garden ; likewise for her final appearance there in 1906. Her beautiful singing in this part was once described as " a miracle of restraint and discretion—never a forced or ill-placed note, never a moment's sacrifice of quality or true colour for the sake of mere sonorousness of effect ". There was a pathetic ring in the last notes of her " Prayer " that brought a tear to every eye.

4

Late in her career she added Kundry to the list of her successes, first of all at Bayreuth, afterwards at New York. But the latter "act of treason", as Frau Cosima termed it, estranged Milka Ternina from Wahnfried for ever. She was a wonderful Kundry. Despite indifferent health (her nerves had become affected some time previously by a slight paralytic seizure), Ternina threw herself into the part with her customary conscientious spirit and energy, and sang the "Herzeleide" with ineffable charm. The New York critics, sticking up for the rights of Bayreuth, had little to say in praise of a superb artistic achievement. Krehbiel in his *Chapters of Opera* ignored everybody and everything except the spectacle; he never mentioned the Kundry.

I met Ternina frequently both in New York and London. She was a woman of singular refinement and obviously superior education. Being intensely musical, she was fond of discussing her art, but would carefully avoid talking about her sister and brother artists or indulging in gossip connected with the operatic stage. She had a profound admiration for the genius of Jean de Reszke, and much regretted that he would never sing Tannhäuser to her Elisabeth; but he could never be induced to attack the rôle. At the same time she claimed that "as Tristan the lover he had never had his equal, while as Siegfried the singer he would never be surpassed". Let me add that so great an Isolde and Brünnhilde as Ternina proved herself worthy to shine beside him; and lucky was the generation that beheld the conjunction of two such supreme artists!

INDEX

R

Lightning Source UK Ltd.
Milton Keynes UK
UKOW052028210113

205178UK00001B/193/A